HOW
TO
BEAT
YOUR ADDICTIONS
AND LIVE A
QUALITY LIFE

HOW TO BEAT

YOUR ADDICTIONS

AND LIVE A

QUALITY LIFE

revised edition

JOHN GIORDANO, C.A.P, MAC, DHL

recovering addict

YorkshirePublishing
www.yorkshirepublishing.com
Write Now.

ISBN: 978-1-947825-51-2
How to Beat Your Addictions and Live a Quality Life
Copyright © 2013 by John Giordano

Yorkshire Publishing
3207 South Norwood Avenue
Tulsa, Oklahoma 74135
www.YorkshirePublishing.com
918.394.2665

· REFLECTIONS ·

DEDICATION

Dedicated to those cold and angry lost souls, who know neither success nor failure, who stand along life's highways watching their lives go by, becoming the effect rather than the cause, blaming everyone else for their misfortunes. May God rescue them from this hell on earth and awaken them to the path of enlightenment!

Acknowledgments

I would like to thank all my contributors, especially my wife, Michele, for their patience and support. Allene Poulk and Dorothy Rodwell, thank you so much for all your help. Thank you to Zena and Rex Lyons for all their assistance in making this manual a reality and to my partners and friends, especially Kenneth Blum, Jerry Goldfarb, Karyn Hurley, and Siobhan Morse, who shared their experience, strength, and hope, which made this book possible. I also want to thank Heather Hale, Lindsay Bockstein, and Alexandria Friedlander for all their hard work and support in this second edition, the editorial and production staff at Tate Publishing for all their help, and to all addicts who have lived and died so that this knowledge could be made available.

CONTENTS

FOREWORD TO FIRST EDITION

This book is an important tool for those seeking to recover from the abuse of numerous substances and behaviors. It is written in a manner that speaks (not preaches) to all, no matter their background or addiction. Its intent is not to confuse or alienate a group but to appeal to a wide range of people. This book reads in a familiar tone as though a friend is talking to you. It is not filled with complicated or sophisticated language so that everyone will gain the fullest understanding of the text. I think John Giordano has been successful in creating a work that will be used and appreciated by all those who read it.

Fritz Jean
Director, New Talent Printing
Miami, Florida

FORWARD TO SECOND EDITION

I first read *Proven Holistic Treatment for Addiction and Chronic Relapse* in 2006 while in treatment at G & G Holistic Addiction Treatment. I knew I had a problem but was certain that it was simply a matter of managing my using. It never occurred to me that I could not only live life free from drugs and alcohol, but really enjoy that life. I found solutions and suggestions in the pages of this book that opened the door for me to a whole new way of life: a life worth living.

In this second edition, we have included the latest evidence-based advances in the art and science of treating addiction and related disorders. We have spent the last five years working closely with the greatest minds in addiction research and treatment, performing original research, and sharing our findings through publications and conference speaking. A list of our scientific publications is included as an appendix.

We have also included a section with success stories because sometimes even when the results are impressive as statistics, we need to hear the human side of things. The stories were volunteered by people who have experienced profound life changes as a result of applying the lessons from this book to their personal lives.

I am a success story as well, thanks to what I have learned from John, this book, and the strategies in this book. I am truly hopeful that you will find what I have found as a result of the methods suggested in this book: a life worth living.

Siobhan A. Morse, MHSA, CRC, CAI, MAC
Former Executive Director
National Institute for
Holistic Addiction Studies

PREFACE

Recovering addicts wrote the words on these pages. In this edition, we have added stories of other addicts and alcoholics. We hope that these can help you identify and understand the importance of the information and suggestions in this book. This information is an accumulation of years of successful continued abstinence from drugs and alcohol. This knowledge was passed down by a number of addicts/alcoholics who have long-term clean time or sobriety and who continually work on their bad character habits. In these pages, you will find some of the excuses addicts use so that they do not have to change. You will also find the antidote for those excuses, learn how to overcome them, and move forward. Some pages suggest that you do some writing or exercise. Please don't take these lightly; they definitely help more than you know.

Do the work, create the change, and enjoy your recovery.

OUR VISION

G & G Holistic Addiction Treatment Program is dedicated to improving treatment outcomes. We investigate new treatment modalities that have the potential to improve treatment outcomes. We are not afraid to think out of the box, especially when someone's life is at stake. Our centers have been designed for those souls who are tormented by their addictions and associated behaviors. The strategies we use are for successful continuous recovery from addictive disorders. Some of our information, methods, treatment, and suggestions are from medical doctors, addictionologists, and psychiatrists. Additional gathered information comes from recovering addicts who were once among the living dead and now share a bond with their Higher Power. We collect data and research all these ideas, suggestions, and methods through our research institute, the National Institute for Holistic Addiction Studies. Maintaining continuous recovery is our goal. Our first priority is a commitment to those who commit to themselves. May God continue to guide us.

Respectfully,
John Giordano, CCJS, MAC, CAP, DHL

John Giordano
786-271-5732
holisticaddictioninfo.com

John's Personal Story

I am a recovering addict who used and abused drugs, alcohol, and anything else that felt good. I was born and raised in New York City, South Bronx, and Harlem. Most of the men in my family, including my father, were in and out of jails and prisons my whole life. I joined and was part of several different ethnic gangs—Black, Hispanic, Irish, and Italian—from the time I was eleven until I was fourteen years old.

When a karate school opened in my neighborhood, some of my friends and I thought we'd go teach the instructor what "tough" really meant. It was I who learned the lesson, and I signed up. By the age of seventeen, I was already the youngest to ever hold the rank of black belt; this was during the days when karate was studied by very few as compared to today. By now though, I had also already quit school—in the beginning of the ninth grade—and had gone to work with an uncle as an apprentice bricklayer. I won the United States karate championship that year, and then I moved to Florida.

Little did I know that I would begin a journey that almost cost me everything, including my life! I started experimenting with drugs and became like two people. One person was a kind and considerate human being, and the other was a self-centered, self-absorbed person who could not take responsibility for his own actions. On the one hand, I owned my own business and had a family; and on the other side, I collected money for smugglers and started to become more like the men in my family.

Becoming famous in the martial arts did not stop me from living a double life. Eventually, the two paths merged, and my life became so dysfunctional that my friends and family did an intervention, and I went to treatment. I didn't go to treatment to get well. I went to get everyone off my back. But something happened while I was in treatment: a spiritual awakening. I realized I could not go on living the way I had been, that I would have to change everything.

It didn't happen overnight. It has been a process, and today I have twenty-seven years of continuous recovery. I received my GED and then went back to school to learn how to help other people like me. I received my certification as an addiction professional (CAP). I became a master addiction counselor (MAC). I became certified as a master of neurolinguistic programming. I also received certifications in hypnotherapy and EMDR. I also went to an alternative church and became a pastor and chaplain for the North Miami Police Department. I've had a hard time believing this myself. I remember hearing the message of recovery beyond my wildest dreams. Wow.

One and a half years into recovery, I raised some money and opened up my first treatment center. Today I am co-owner of a treatment center that specializes in evidence-based holistic treatment of dual diagnosis and chronic relapse. I designed this treatment program to deal with the whole person: mind, body, and spirit. We utilize cutting-edge twenty-first-century technologies that address the entire human being: mind, body, and spirit.

I have been blessed; I haven't relapsed since I got clean and sober twenty-seven years ago, even though it was not always easy to stay clean and sober. I suffered many consequences. Some of the hardest times in my life were when I had to watch my children go through the pain of active addiction. I know the feelings of helplessness that family members feel and the guilt that goes with it, especially the fear of the possibility of them dying. I remember watching my son lay in a hospital bed getting his stomach pumped because he had overdosed. I was crying and blaming myself. Even though I had some years of recovery under my belt, I still felt these overwhelming feelings of guilt and shame. Thank God for my recovery support group reminding me that it wasn't my fault and to remember to let go and let God. The work and years of experience paid off.

Today, thank God, my family is intact and doing well. My children are also in recovery. My life has changed beyond my wildest dreams. This book is a way of sharing my experience, strength, and hope with everyone who struggles with this insidious disease.

May a higher power continue
To bless us all
With love and gratitude

John J. Giordano
"A Grateful Recovering Addict"

Looking outside myself never gave me
what I was looking for. Only when I
looked inside did I find my truth!

Here are some slogans that I hated. But today I live by them—how ironic!

◊ Drugs and alcohol are bad for you.
◊ Give time time, and be consistent.
◊ It works if you work it, so work it. You are worth it.
◊ If you change your response, you will change your outcome.
◊ Nothing changes if nothing changes.
◊ Life is what you make it.
◊ Today is the first day of the rest of your new life.
◊ Recovery is a process, not an event.
◊ If you do what you always did, you will get what you always got.
◊ Let go and let God.
◊ It is what it is.

Some men say, That!!!!!!!!!!!!!!
To have a Lady by your side
Will make you strong and make you High,
She will even help you to obtain the Sky.
But? Her price, my friend, is quite HIGH!!!!
For she takes away the light of Day,
And sends you on your merry way.........
For her first undertaking is in breaking.
She'll make you bend and lose conception
Of who's your friend.
Her Philosophy is quite strong
She teaches you that nothing is wrong.
That whatever you do
There is always a good reason to!
Now! There's her daughter Miss Paranoia
Whose strength is so great,
That it even rattles God's very gate.
And teaches men how to lose their fate
And replace it with a terrible Hate!!!!
For these poor souls who once stood so bold
Now stand all alone and are tired and cold.
For they have sold their soul,
For a bag of white GOLD
And riches untold.
MAY GOD SEND THEM GRACE!!!!!!!
So she may rescue them from space,
and make them men again and a friend
AGAIN.

AMEN
By John G

Holistic Addiction Treatment for the Twenty-First Century

ABOUT ADDICTION

A number of factors contribute to the development of addictive behaviors, such as genetics, early childhood trauma, mental illness, family history, inner and environment. There is a clinical distinction between addiction and occasional, limited use of an abusable drug. Of the twenty-nine million American adults who try an illicit substance, nearly six million will go on to abuse drugs and alcohol and become addicted.

There are several schools of thought about what has us start using drugs or alcohol to begin with. I do not think that there is only one reason that things happen. Why we used is not as important as what we are going to do to get better; but sometimes understanding the process that had us start can also help us stop.

Some of us used because it was what our peers were doing. We have all heard the term "peer pressure." That doesn't mean that we would have lost all our friends or our social status if we had not taken that drink or maybe had that hit of marijuana, but it does mean that we felt somehow that we would be alone or different if we did not do what others were doing. The pressure usually came from that inner voice we hear when we are alone or feeling alone. Although there may be some of us who were pressured by others to use, peer pressure does not mean that the pressure really came from others but, in fact, came from within us.

Some of us first began using because a doctor prescribed the medication to us. This is happening more and more these days. Between 2001 and 2004, 47 percent of all persons in the United States used at least one prescription drug in the past month. Most of these people are taking medicines only for the reasons the medications were prescribed; however, an estimated 20 percent of people in the United States have used prescription drugs for nonmedical reasons. According to the National Institute on Drug Abuse (NIDA), in 2006 16.2 million Americans age twelve and older had taken a prescription pain reliever, tranquilizer, stimulant, or sedative for nonmedical purposes at least once in the year prior to begin surveyed" (National Survey on Drug Use and Health, http://www.samhsa.gov/).

Experts don't know exactly why this type of drug abuse is increasing. There are many factors, including the ease of access through online pharmacies, the development of new and very strong drugs by the pharmaceutical companies, and the shortening length of time that doctors actually spend with patients. The key point here is that anyone can become addicted.

> *I was diagnosed with migraines and given a pain prescription at 9 years old. By 10 years old, I was sneaking pain pills out of the medicine cabinet even when I didn't need them. Years later, I lost a baby and was given pain medication again. I used the medication so I didn't have to face my feelings and my fears. When I was later diagnosed with Lupus and again given a legitimate reason to take pain medications, I was no longer able to control my using. More and more I turned to the pain medication to help me through the day, always thinking, "Tomorrow I won't take any, tomorrow will be a better day."*
>
> Marcy U, Recovering Addict

At some point in the use of a legitimate prescription, the person who becomes addicted trades other coping mechanisms for the one that seems to be working. After all, why would you fix something that is not broken? Regardless of whether the pain is physical or psychological, the addiction cycle has begun.

Early childhood trauma includes sexual and physical abuse, neglect, or abandonment, and it is often associated with the development of mental illnesses. Several mental illnesses tend to co-occur with substance abuse. Some of the more common mental illnesses that accompany addiction disorders include learning disabilities, attention deficit disorder, bipolar disorder, anxiety disorders, and depression. Addictions are often developed through an attempt to alleviate the symptoms of these illnesses. The 2001 NHSDA report states that among adults with mental illness in 2001, 20.3 percent (about three million people) were dependent on or abusing alcohol or illicit drugs. The rate among adults without serious mental illnesses was about 6 percent.

Even events later in life such as those that might lead to post-traumatic stress disorder can lead to substance abuse. These events might be a single, very traumatic event that happened or even low levels of chronic stress due to family or other environmental factors. Similarly, physical trauma, such as a severe blow to the head, is associated with increased addiction and substance abuse rates.

Psychological pain is no less significant or important than physical pain. Sometimes physical pain is easier to identify or recognize, but psychological pain can be just as debilitating. Psychological pain can be caused by past traumas, such as in post-traumatic stress disorder (PTSD). PTSD is usually thought to be associated with a single or short, but extreme experience, such as being raped or being a victim of other violence or from a war experience. This is not always the case. David and Merlene Miller (2002) described situations of low level, but prolonged stress that can also cause PTSD and associated disorders.

Family history of addiction or mental illness is also a very important factor. Certain genetic factors that are attributed to behavior may be passed down from generation to generation. Recent research demonstrates that the existence of certain factors in your genetic profile can increase the likelihood of becoming addicted. While there are new tests that are just coming into the mainstream marketplace, one of the simplest ways to determine genetic predisposition is to look at immediate family. The more family members that had problems with alcohol, gambling, or even severe anger issues, the more likely that there is a genetic factor at work in the family.

More research is demonstrating that there is a genetic component to addictions. Some individuals are born with variations in the reward pathways in their brain. There are variations that result in a reduced ability to experience pleasure, to control impulses, and to manage strong emotions such as anger. In these cases, using at first may actually help us feel better. This applies to using prescribed substances, drugs, and alcohol. A significant problem is that using also causes chemical imbalances. Once the delicate chemical balances in the brain deviate from normal, whether it begins with a genetic disorder or it happens through using chemicals, the body and the brain do their best to adapt and establish a new normal.

Often these genetic variations—not abnormalities, variations—result in the use and eventual abuse of substances such as alcohol and drugs and processes such as gambling or sex addictions.

Genetics is also further influenced by the physical environment surrounding the individual. Some parents and caretakers develop their addictions at an early age and never learn to cope with adversity. Their inability to utilize appropriate coping skills is then taught to those they care for, thereby propagating their addictive behavior. As with all addictive behaviors, as these individuals grow older, these behaviors become more deeply rooted, and their addiction grows stronger until it becomes more difficult to satisfy.

Regardless of why we started, at some point, we feel like we have found the best way to get through life. Some of us feel like we have made a conscious decision to use, and some of us feel like we were trapped. The result is the same. We become enslaved by the disease of addiction.

Addiction can destroy a human being on every level of their existence. It damages them mentally, emotionally, physically, and spiritually, leaving them virtually drowning in a sea of loneliness and despair. The hope that they may one day win their battle to stop using vanishes completely. They lose touch with their Higher Power, and their life becomes a seemingly endless series of failures, which eventually leads to total yielding to their addiction and their pain. People suffering from addiction not only abuse drugs and alcohol but also every person, place, and thing with whom they come in contact. Although it is not their intention to cause such tumultuous pain in those around them, their battered emotions seep into all areas of their lives, making attempts at recovery futile.

While in the pages of this book we are dealing primarily with the diagnosable conditions referred to as substance abuse disorders including drug addiction and alcoholism, and to some extent, process abuse disorders, it should be noted that there are much larger definitions of addiction in use today as well. Addiction can be seen as a loss of balance. We lose control, and we lose ourselves. In addiction, we lose our sense of self and our connectedness to others.

Addiction is demonstrated in the lengths to which we go to get what we believe we need. And while this may be the demonstration, it therefore is also the manifestation of the depth of the pain we are in during active addiction.

Regardless of whether you are in full-blown active addiction and looking for a way out or if you are trapped by a partner or loved one's addiction or if you simply wish to recover from some unhealthy habits that crept up for you over time, this book can help. In these pages, you will find many ways to support your recovery regardless of what you are recovering from. And in your heart, you will find the why to recover. So give yourself a break, and let's begin.

THE HOLISTIC APPROACH

In years past, addiction and co-occurring mental health treatment has focused primarily on treating the psychological aspects of the disease of addiction while neglecting to address the delicate interconnective balance of the body, mind, and spirit. Most individuals who enter into a twenty-eight-day treatment program receive education about their addiction that only scratches the surface of the underlying issues of their addictive behavior and are introduced to a twelve-step program addressing their particular set of symptoms. After treatment, clients are encouraged to live in a supportive environment such as a three-quarter-way house. However, most return to their homes unprepared to live a life without drugs. In some cases, this traditional approach to treatment may be effective. Usually, the success rate of traditional addiction treatment is very low.

The wisdom of western medicine is that if you have a symptom, treat it. If a person has a headache, they take ibuprofen or acetaminophen to alleviate the symptoms. But they almost never determine the root cause of the headache. The holistic approach holds that human beings have a body, a mind, and a spirit. These elements of the human being are intertwined and exist in a state of constant flux, seeking balance by reacting to changes in the internal and external environment. The body's ability to self-regulate in its tendency toward balance determines an individual's level of health in all aspects: physical (body), psychological (mind), and spiritual (spirit). The holistic method approaches treatment with the understanding that balance must be restored.

An exciting new detox treatment that deals primarily with painless detox from drugs and alcohol, known as Ibogaine, has experienced particular success in the holistic approach to treatment. This treatment is used for the detox of alcohol, opiates, heroin, and methadone. Typically, it takes about seven days to three months to detox an individual who is addicted to heroin or methadone. Detox treatment with ibogaine takes between 24-36 hours, with little to no side effects.

Ibogaine is a rain forest alkaloid derived from the root of the Tabernanthe iboga (Apocynacea family), which is a shrub indigenous to the West Central Africa. Ibogaine is used by the native people in low doses to relive fatigue, hunger, and thirst. The pharmacogenic effects of Ibogaine have been researched for over 100 years. The anti-addictive properties of Ibogaine were first reported in 1982.

People who are substance-dependent have stated that Ibogaine treatment puts them into a waking dream state. These Ibogaine-induced dreams are usually centered on early childhood traumas and other important developmental events that occurred during turning points in their life. Once awaked from these dream-like visions, insights into interpreting the root cause of their addictive personalities are often revealed. At the end of the Ibogaine treatment, opiates, alcohol, and cocaine dependent individuals experienced some relief or the total cessation of the drug or alcohol craving. Also, opiate-dependent clients stated that their opiate withdrawal symptoms were alleviated.

Dr. Deborah Mash from the University of Miami, funded under NIDA (National Institute of Drug Addiction), is a Neuroscientist and Chief researcher of the Ibogaine Project. Dr. Mash has been in collaboration with me for the last ten years to create a new holistic treatment approach to addiction that is more effective than current methodologies. This alliance formed to treat drug abuse encompasses Ibogaine treatment along with other modalities that work cooperatively to restore healthy body, mind and spirit functioning.

RESTORING THE BODY

The twenty-first-century holistic approach begins first with the body. What we ingest creates the foundation for the proper functioning of our mind and body. Stimulants and toxins such as caffeine, refined sugars, processed foods, food additives, and a poor overall diet contribute immensely to an imbalance in brain chemistry. It is crucial that these foods and additives be eliminated or significantly reduced in the diet in order to restore healthy brain functioning. In exchange, a complete eating plan consisting of fruit, fiber, fish, turkey, whole grains, protein, and lots of water must be embraced.

Those entering treatment may be dehydrated, hypo/hyperglycemic, and protein deficient. A total of 80 percent have heavy metal toxicity that can cause depression and anxiety. They also need to be evaluated for certain bacterial and fungal infections, such as *Candida albicans* and H pylori. Chemical dependency along with an insufficient diet can wreak havoc in an individual's delicate immune system. These complications can contribute to depression, agitation, decreased energy stores, and eventually, relapse.

Along with a proper meal plan, a good vitamin supplement and amino acid regiment are also necessary. Much of the vitamin, mineral, and amino acid stores, which are the building blocks of neurotransmitters in the brain, are depleted from drug and alcohol abuse. Also, exercise, meditation, neurofeedback, and stress-reduction techniques are essential in keeping the mind and body stable. Some excellent disciplines for achieving mind/body congruency are yoga, tai chi, karate, and meditation.

Acupuncture is a modality that can often assist the body in the rebalancing process. This treatment allows energy to flow properly to stimulate the production of neurotransmitters and calm some of the cravings for drugs and alcohol. Also, nurturing the body with hot baths and steams, good music, and gentle relaxation will help to rid the body of toxins and stress and restore peace of mind.

RESTORING THE MIND

Current research has suggested that certain chemical imbalances in the brain appear to play an important role in contributing to addiction. The use and abuse of drugs and alcohol causes brain chemistry to deviate even further from the normal range. The 2001 NHSDA reported that those who use illicit drugs were twice as likely to have serious mental illnesses as compared with those adults who did not abuse illicit drugs. With chronic abuse, a vicious cycle is formed, which grows exponentially over time. This causes a lack of concentration, emotional instability, feelings of depression, and a total absence of a moral and spiritual balance. In many cases, medication, and nutraceuticals are necessary to correct the chemical imbalance resulting from mental illnesses. For some who suffer chronic relapse, psychotropic medication or amino acid therapy is an integral part of their recovery. It is of paramount importance to change the root causes of the addictive behavior in order for treatment to be successful. Some effective new therapies that can effectuate tremendous changes in behavior are EMDR, TRT, NLP, and neurofeedback, as well as amino acid therapy and nutraceuticals treatment.

Eye movement desensitization and reprocessing (EMDR) is an approach to psychotherapy that uses eye movements to stimulate the information processing in the brain. A recent study performed by Kaiser-Permanente found that EMDR was twice as effective as typical therapy. At our treatment center, we have developed an advanced, quicker, and more effective version called TRT—trauma relief therapy. This therapy provides much faster results than traditional therapy and standard EMDR. It is used for treating trauma such as sexual abuse, domestic violence, victims of war and crime, depression, addiction, phobias, and self-esteem issues. We have found TRT to be effective for overcoming sleep disorders as well as overcoming performance anxiety and performance slumps. Overall, TRT allows the brain heal "sick" thinking patterns in a single session, thus making a long and tedious recovery a thing of the past. TRT incorporates NLP, EMDR, and hypnotherapy, which makes it very effective

Another interesting modality that is very effective is neurolinguistic programming (NLP). NLP is the study of the structure of subjective experience. It is a therapeutic tool that can reprogram a client's belief systems and behaviors. NLP incorporates a set of models on how communication can be affected by subjective experience. It utilizes a change in language and thought processes to understand behaviors. Simply put, it teaches you how to model success.

Hypnotherapy uses imagery, guided meditation, and suggestions to help achieve a focused state of heightened concentration similar to a trance. The hypnotic state allows the client to explore painful experiences and uncomfortable emotions that they might have blocked from memory. In this way, hypnotherapy supports the psychotherapy process. Other uses for hypnotherapy are smoking cessation and behavior modification. There is also evidence that hypnotherapy can be used effectively in pain management.

Neurofeedback is a cutting-edge technique that trains the brain in order to help it improve body function regulation and overall brain health. When there is poor brain functioning, it is recognized through the EEG (electroencephalogram). By challenging the brain, much like when muscles are challenged in physical exercise to improve their strength, normal brain functionality can be restored. The benefits of neurofeedback include developing healthier sleep patterns, obtaining relief from anxiety and depression, and enhancing mental attention and emotional balance. Emotional management is very important in how an individual reacts to a particular situation.

Some of the most exciting advances in addiction treatment relate to repairing the brain. All the treatments that attempt to change thinking or behavior patterns and encourage new beliefs and thoughts are dependent on a healthy, functioning brain. Research has demonstrated that brain repair is possible. For years medicine taught that brain cells damaged by drugs, alcohol, trauma, stroke, and other physically catastrophic events were dead and lost. Recently, however, it has been determined that often these cells are not dead; they are inactive. There are treatments that can support the reactivation of these cells such as hyperbaric oxygen therapy, nutraceuticals, and nutrition therapy, all of which are discussed in this book.

RESTORING THE SPIRIT

One of the most important steps in recovery is psychological awareness. Becoming aware of personal speech, thoughts, body language, and actions is crucial in maintaining a life free from chemical dependency. It is important to learn how to avoid the pitfalls of negative thoughts and negative people. An individual must learn that it is more important to be kind than to be right, to develop values and integrity, and finally, to learn to be good to oneself and others by trusting in a Higher Power.

By believing in a Higher Power, it is easier to submit oneself to recovery and treatment. The relationship that is developed through spirituality enriches life and gives hope and inspiration. Recovering individuals discover that a life free from the clutches of drugs and alcohol is not only possible, but it is a life well worth living. Spirituality is the foundation for the development of a positive living philosophy.

Twelve-step programs are a spiritual way of life. They are nondenominational, anonymous, and noncontroversial. The success of these programs is based upon "the therapeutic value of one addict helping another." Many atheist and agnostic individuals have been able to embrace the twelve steps with their own personal concept of a Higher Power. The role of a Higher Power in their life becomes G. O. D. (good orderly direction). Every addict that is serious about recovery is able to attain serenity and fullness of life by applying these steps and these principles to their daily life.

DRUGS, ALCOHOL, AND THE BRAIN

The human brain is the most complex organ in the body. Weighing in at about three pounds, it is the center for everything we think, do, and feel; it shapes everything we experience—every thought, emotion, and behavior. Quantum physics will even tell you that it plays a role in creating reality.

The brain is three pounds of pure power made up of many parts that work together, coordinating to perform specific functions.

An example is this: Right now you are reading these words because electrical and chemical messages are being sent from one area to another. Your heart is beating at a resting rate, and you are breathing in a relaxed manner because your cerebral cortex is communicating with your brain stem that there is no danger, and your forebrain is then freed up to interpret the words on this page. Simultaneously, your limbic system is interpreting emotional stimuli, and you are experiencing these emotions as your mood.

Areas of the Brain Affected by Drug and Alcohol Abuse

Brain Stem – this area of the brain is responsible for the activities necessary to stay alive; such as breathing, heart beat and sleep.

Limbic System – also call the Reward System, this part of the brain is actually a number of structures linked together to control and regulate our ability to experience pleasure. When we experience pleasure by performing a certain activity, we are motivated by a desire to repeat the activity. Eating activates our pleasure system as does reproductive behavior. Both these activities are necessary for species survival. Using drugs and alcohol or process addictions such as gambling or internet porn, also stimulate the limbic system. The limbic system also plays a role in emotional perception and mood.

Cerebral Cortex – this area processes all incoming data from our senses and then is responsible for interpreting it and reacting to it. The front part of the cerebral cortex, called the frontal cortex, is where we think, plan and make decisions.

Someone who just did cocaine is having a significantly different experience from someone who did not. The cocaine tricks the brain into communicating a completely different message. Heroin, on the other hand, would interfere with the brain's ability to communicate altogether.

The brain uses chemicals called neurotransmitters to communicate. Dr. Ken Blum, cofounder of the alcoholic gene, describes this natural phenomenon: "Structure deep within the limbic system play a crucial role in the expression of emotions and the activity of the reward system of the brain. The experience of pleasure is based on a reward 'cascade'...that interact through various signaling molecules, or neurotransmitters...a deficiency in one or more of these neurons or signaling molecules can supplant [or replace] an individual's feeling of well-being with anxiety, anger or a craving for a substance that can alleviate the negative emotion."

Some drugs, such as cocaine and amphetamines, cause large releases of the brain's natural neurotransmitters while other substances such as heroin and marijuana actually mimic neurotransmitters. Alcohol and process addictions, like sex and gambling, also impact the brain's ability to manufacture, send, receive, and process these chemical messengers. All addictions are a result of a substance or process causing a flood in the brain's reward system.

With continued alcohol or drug use, the brain will compensate for the false surges in neurotransmitters by either producing less of the neurotransmitters, which are chemicals in the brain that control mood, or by reducing the area or space on the brain where the neurotransmitters can have an effect. The result is flatness, depression, anxiety, or other negative mood state, which the user feels when they do not have enough of the substance.

One of the most difficult challenges of recovery is overcoming the negative feelings associated with the damage done to the neurotransmitter systems. One of the goals of this book is to educate people about the many holistic ways that we can help to heal the brain and reduce symptoms and cravings and create a strong relapse prevention program.

CHANGING YOUR LIFE

Change

In early recovery, everything may seem overwhelming, very difficult, and like a lot of work. It will appear boring and repetitive, and your life will seem to be lonely and frustrating, but as long as you follow suggestions, these feelings will pass. Change is frightening, but as soon as you overcome your fears and look back, you'll realize that it wasn't such a big deal.

Recovery is discovering who you are and who you can become. You can change your life to become all that our Creator intended us to be— loving, productive human beings. Don't be afraid to ask for help. Anyone who has maintained any length of time in recovery sought help and obviously got what they needed. The only thing you must change is everything. If you do not change, the only thing that will is your clean date. So give yourself some time—how much time is up to our Higher Power and us. Our life begins when we say it does. So say it. Remember God gave us the gift of life; it's what we do with that life that is our gift back to the Creator.

VALUES AND PRINCIPLES

Create a list of the things you value, for example, recovery, spirituality, family relationships, work/career, life, my body, open communication with others, etc. After creating this list of values, prioritize them in order of importance. Every day, take a look at your list and see if you compromised—or failed to honor—any of your values. If you did, ask yourself, "What do I need to do to avoid that in the future?" and take action. Recognize and remember the difference between how you feel when you uphold your values and how you feel when you don't. Honor yourself and your values because if you don't, you will create low self-esteem and an environment to use and abuse. This leads to a life of misery and despair.

A good place to start defining your own values and principles is your twelve-step program. Some sponsors say there is a principle for each step. Here is a list that was given to me when I got clean:

Step 1 – Honesty
Step 2 – Hope
Step 3 – Faith
Step 4 – Courage
Step 5 – Integrity
Step 6 – Willingness
Step 7 – Humility
Step 8 – Brotherly Love
Step 9 – Self Discipline

How to Beat Your Addictions and Live a Quality Life

Step 10 – Perseverance
Step 11 – Spirituality
Step 12 – Service

JOURNALING

Keep a journal. Buy a small wired note pad that fits in your shirt pocket, and write down your reactions to various situations and feelings that you may have experienced during the day. By reading your journal every night, you will start to see a pattern of how your thoughts caused you to react both positively and negatively. After a week, go back over your journal and start to alter the behaviors that you want to change. After doing this for a while, you will be amazed at how much progress you can make in changing your thought patterns and the way you respond to situations.

When we do drugs or alcohol, we lose touch with our true self. Journaling will help you to rid yourself of negative thoughts and learn another way of thinking and acting. This will be beneficial for you and the people around you. Recovery is about self-discovery and change.

BOREDOM

Each day, do your best to challenge yourself. Do something different for fun, do something relaxing, or do something you've never done before. When you're bored, it's because you're boring. Get up and participate in life; don't have contempt prior to investigation. If you feel lonely, don't stay alone; change where you are, get busy, call a friend, call your sponsor, go to a meeting, or help another recovering addict. Do something productive, and stop playing the role of the victim. Deal with life, or life will deal with you.

Addicts in general seem to always want some kind of action, some drama in their lives. The problem is that we mistake serenity for boredom and choose unhealthy ways to create excitement in our lives. When we invest our time wisely, we no longer confuse serenity and boredom.

SPIRITUALITY

Spirituality is not religion. There are no rules in spirituality. You can believe in anything that helps you stay clean and live a powerful life. It is suggested that you find a Power Greater than yourself that is also loving and caring. This is all you need to begin a relationship with a Higher Power.

Spirituality can be a great refuge from pain and suffering. A Higher Power seems to be present in recovering people with long-term abstinence.

Spirituality is not only about believing in something. Spirituality is about how we live our lives. An example is being kind instead of being right. Do your best not to lie, cheat, or steal. Help others.

Also remember, recovery is about progress, not perfection. No one is perfect, at least no one on this planet.

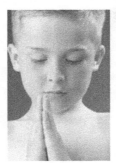

MEDITATION

Meditation is the key to the locked doorway of your subconscious mind. It will open it up and let you take a look at your unresolved issues. Meditation will also help you learn to slow your racing thoughts and relax. Research shows that meditation supports the production and use of chemicals in the brain that help us feel good. Meditation has been used to help overcome chronic pain, aid in sleeping better, and reduce anxiety and stress.

There are many ways to meditate. Use the Internet to find different types of meditation. There are also various CDs and books available on the topic. Some CDs will guide you in your meditation. Guided meditations are helpful in beginning the practice of meditation.

Meditate morning and night to center yourself. Here is an example: Sit with your back straight, and breathe in slowly through your nose and out of your mouth. While meditating, don't worry about being fidgety or about thoughts flying all around, just focus on your breathing and say to yourself, "In and out." Imagine an open door on your right temple and one on your left. Then see your thoughts going in and going out and just focus on your breathing. Do this for at least five minutes every day and every night. Slowly increase your meditation to thirty minutes; this is not a requirement, just a suggestion. It takes time, hard work, and especially patience, but the rewards outweigh the hard work ten to one. Don't forget, people all over the world have been using meditation for centuries.

I believe that this too shall pass. The alternative is jails, institutions, or death. This time I choose recovery.

UNMANAGEABILITY

Addiction is a behavior done continuously in spite of reoccurring adverse consequences. Addiction hides in a multitude of behaviors besides just drinking and drugging. Gambling, spending, sex, relationships, work, exercise, and food are just a few examples.

Moderation and sometimes abstinence is necessary. Stopping the drinking or drugging is only the first step in the recovery process. You must learn that when it comes to your addiction and your life becomes unmanageable, you are powerless.

If you are not consistent, nothing will ever change unless you seek the proper help. Alone against your addiction, you are sure to lose, but together nothing can stop us. Don't reinvent the wheel; follow directions of people who are the winners, those who have maintained a life free of drugs and alcohol, and that includes any other behaviors that cause us to become out of balance.

When we are willing and committed to doing the work that is suggested, our "wants" are no longer obsessions.

WORK ADDICTION

Be careful of work addiction; it will get you every time. Yes, we must pay our bills. Yes, we need to feed our families. Yes, we have to pay back those debts. Yes, we owe it to our employer. But these are all the reasons that work addiction throws people off the path of recovery, and it is a sure relapse. Priorities start to change; you find other things becoming more important than your recovery, but at what price? Recovery is about balance; it is about first things first, and recovery is definitely first.

If you don't overcome your addiction, there is no job, which means no money. You will not be able to pay those bills or feed the family, so who are you trying to kid? How come you didn't care about it when you were drinking or drugging?

Yes, in the beginning, things may not happen as fast as you would like, and you may lose some things, but anything is possible if you stay clean and sober. You have a disease of "I want it now" and "I want more." Recovery teaches us patience, tolerance, and gratitude for what we do have. I would like to think, "No pain, no gain."

In the beginning, start slowly. Do not take on too many responsibilities at the same time. Do not work long hours. Early in recovery, do your best not to work more than thirty hours a week. Slow down, and you will get much more accomplished. Life is a journey, not a race. Do this for a minimum of one year, and if nothing changes, we will gladly refund your misery.

I'm not like these people. I have plenty of money. I don't understand why they keep telling me I'm in denial.

MONEY OBSESSION

Now, let's talk about people who are able to get back all they lost and become successful in early recovery. Here is my take on it. Addicts who are capable of making lots of money quickly have trouble with honesty and humility. They get caught up in the frenzy of making money , and lo and behold, they are using again. Because they are resourceful and creative, money comes relatively easy. Addicts are addicted to quick money and easy pickings and are easily distracted from their primary purpose, which is to live along spiritual lines.

Rapid success can lead to rapid failure. Self-centeredness and self-importance will cause them to lose humility and willingness to change. Be careful of these pitfalls. There is a solution! We have to change our ways. change is hard, but with the help of meetings, the steps, and a sponsor, we can do it. Stay grounded, work a program of honesty and humility, and don't take the easy way out. A good therapist should be used for these underlying issues. I believe in covering all my bases. If you want to be a winner, do the work. You will definitely get the job done.

LONELINESS AND EMPTINESS

We all feel lonely or empty at one time or another. It just means that we are human. Addicts are used to fixing these feelings by using something or someone. But those solutions never work for long.

Loneliness or emptiness can also be a sign that we need to work on our spiritual program. A way to remedy these feelings of despair is to create a gratitude list. If we open our eyes, we can see that we are never alone or empty when we allow others in, including our Higher Power. Get over the "poor me" attitude and enjoy whatever life you *do* have. Remember you're only alone because you choose to be.

You're *not* alone. Allow yourself to reach out.

My life is too good. I will succeed.

You are NOT Alone

If you came from an alcoholic or drug-using family, learn how it may have affected your personality and the way you deal or don't deal with life. You can do some research on adult children of alcoholics (ACOA). It doesn't matter whether it is drugs or alcohol; the results are all the same.

There is a valuable book that can help: *Adult Children of Alcoholics Syndrome*. (See the bibliography.) This may help you realize that there is hope in your life and that you are not alone. Each addiction has a specific set of symptoms, and all of them are interrelated. Some of the books I suggest you read are listed in the bibliography.

After reading the suggested literature, you should have a pretty good handle on what to do in order to live a full and rewarding life. Information is great, but without action, it is meaningless. So begin your new life now. God knows you have earned it. Action begins by following directions—not your own. So what are you waiting for? Go for it! If I did it, so can you.

I don't want to relapse.

LIVING IN THE PAST AND FUTURE

People who are addicted tend to live and dwell in the past, often skipping over the present. This leads to recreating past fears in their future. This becomes habitual, and we don't even know we are doing it. This thinking and behavior causes us to recreate our past pains and reexperience them over and over and over and over.

By working the twelve steps of AA/NA/ GA/OA, we can learn to live in the present and begin to realize that what we do in the present creates our future. This is how change works. Our past is from where we draw our experience. There are no failures, only lessons. So stop living in your past because if you don't, you won't have a future worth living.

When we live in the future, we get overwhelmed: "I'm not going to get this," "I'm not going to have that," "I'm not going to be successful." Doing this, we miss the chance to change. Most things we wanted badly enough, we got, regardless of the obstacles. When we really wanted to use, we got the job done, didn't we? Live in the now, and create the new you and your new future. To stay in the present, look toward your future, and learn from your history. This will help you be successful.

No recovery, no life worth living.

MEETINGS

Self-help groups such as AA/NA/GA/OA[1] suggest ninety meetings in ninety days. It is important to get a sponsor, preferably someone with at least three years of recovery, who has worked the steps and is still active in the program. This way, they can help you avoid the pitfalls of recovery. Going to AA/NA/GA/OA is an ordeal for some. They don't like the people, the place, the smoke, etc., but this is normal because we don't like change.

Learn to acquire a taste for the meetings. Take the meat and leave the bones.

Examine where you ended up when you drank or used drugs. Did you ever look at the people you were hanging out with? It is very important to be around other people with similar problems who are also fighting to rebuild their lives. Find the winners and get close to them; learn what helped them so you can help yourself. Find a meeting place where you feel most comfortable. If you don't find one, keep searching until you do. Don't give up. Remember, you went to any lengths to get your drug of choice. Now do the same to get your recovery.

GOAL SETTING

Goal setting is very important because it creates a zest for life and builds your confidence. Start small. Set short-term goals and then long-term goals. Keep in mind your main focus is on your recovery. When you complete one of your goals, be proud and give yourself a reward. You need to be careful when you are working on your goals.

Beware of being too compulsive or obsessive. This will burn you out, and you will not want to finish the job.

Please slow down and take it easy. It took a long time to get sick, and it will take time to get well. When you wanted to use, you had a plan, gathered all your resources, and then went to any length to get the job done. So don't tell yourself, "I can't!" "I don't know how!" "I don't know what I want to do!" These are all excuses you never used when you wanted to get high. So get busy, create a life you can be proud of, and go for it!

BODY LANGUAGE

Become aware of how you sit and stand because body language has a lot to do with how you feel. Stand and sit up straight. Don't slump. Do you remember when others would tell us this and how we hated it? Funny thing, what was told to us is quite valid. When your vertebra are straight, your energy flows smoothly and uninterrupted. When you walk with your head up, you carry a sense of confidence, you are sure of yourself, and your energy is flowing smoothly. This will assist you in having a better sense of well-being.

When you sit or walk with your head down or your posture is all twisted, you're telling yourself and people that something is wrong and you are not okay. This can and does block smooth energy flow. So be aware of your posture.

BREATHING

Most people never think about how they breathe or just take it for granted. Learn to breathe deeply from below your navel, breathing slowly in and out. By breathing slowly and deeply, you help calm yourself in times of stress. Posture and breathing are very important, so please don't take them for granted. Awareness helps our lives become more manageable. When you're very upset and things aren't going your way, remember to slow your breathing down so you can then more clearly get to the best solution for the situation.

SELF-TALK

Be careful of how you talk to yourself. Never put yourself down or call yourself stupid, lazy, etc. This is called negative self-talk. When you do this, repeat to yourself, "Cancel, cancel, cancel." Do your best not to say negative statements about yourself or anyone else because this brings negative energy back to you.

If you find yourself obsessed on using drugs or alcohol or having any behavior that is not going to benefit you in recovery, change where you are, call someone, and immediately do something to create movement. Don't allow your negative self-talk to keep talking.

When you focus on negative thoughts, stop and do your best to replace the negative with positive because if you don't, your negative thoughts will soon come alive. Stop playing helpless. Take charge of your feelings, or they will take charge of you. Positive self-talk helps more than you will ever know.

POSITIVE AFFIRMATIONS

Positive affirmations are a very good way to reinforce your positive thinking. I suggest you buy those little post-it notes and write down some positive affirmations. Place these little stickies on your bathroom mirror, by your dresser, or in prominent places. Here are a few affirmations you may want to consider: "Be kind," "This too shall pass," "Get out of yourself," "Stay focused," and my favorite, "Gratitude instead of attitude." Don't judge it; just do it and see if it works for you!

EXPECTATIONS

When we expect something and don't get it, we may be disappointed. Often this starts the process of beating ourselves up and dragging all our failures to the present. Then we play the victim and the *poor me* attitude starts. You will eventually medicate yourself with food, sex, work, exercise, money, etc.—anything not to feel or think. Instead of medicating yourself, you need to enjoy the journey and not be attached to the result.

Here is the addict's favorite song: "If only I had done that," "If only she/he would be different," "If only my family understood what I'm going through," and on and on. Enough with the song—you're right where you need to be. All you have to do is give time time, be consistent, and build a strong foundation in recovery. Build a powerful support system, and continue to reach out to the winners, asking them how they felt early in recovery. Find out what people did or how they stopped putting expectations on other people and themselves. If you keep asking, sooner or later, you'll find your truth, and it will set you free.

PROJECTION

Leave projection to the people who work with crystal balls. We love to project, and often it doesn't come out the way we expected. Because things didn't happen fast enough, didn't happen at all, or happened and it wasn't what we expected, we get angry with everyone, ourselves included. So when you project outcomes, it usually never turns out the way you want. Then you work yourself up and get stressed out over something that has not even happened.

The future is up to your Higher Power, not you. Do as much as you can and let go of your obsession because if you hold on to it, you will eventually get sick or high. Being obsessed with the outcome and thinking you are sure you know what is going to happen can create unwarranted fears. Stay grounded by meditating, talking to your Higher Power, and enjoying the journey. You never know when your journey will end. If you learn to stay at peace within yourself the best you can and as often as you can, you then learn to live life one day at a time and sometimes one moment at a time with a positive attitude.

RESENTMENTS

Resentments can only hurt us, not help. Reliving anger and pain and displacing it on other people will only cause us to become depressed and more angry. Next, we will use a substance to ease the pain. We can't change people, places, or things, but we can change ourselves and how we respond to situations. Self-righteousness never worked for anyone who was successful in recovery.

We love to be forgiven for our misdeeds, but we just about refuse to forgive others.

If you do not share about what you are feeling and how you allowed someone to get under your skin, resentments will be created. All you have to do is talk to your Higher Power and ask for help and guidance. Say the serenity prayer: "God, grant me the serenity to accept the things I can not change, the courage to change the things I can, and the wisdom to know the difference." You can't change that person, but you can change yourself, and knowing this is the difference. I know you're probably saying, "Yeah, sure!" Let's look at some options.

We can ruin a good time, a relationship, a job, a career, and who knows what else, but you don't have to sabotage your serenity over something you cannot change. Learn to forgive if you want to attract forgiveness. That is what it is all about.

ANGER

Addicts and alcoholics are often addicted to excitement and adrenaline rushes. Anger is a primary example of one feeling an addict knows and knows well. When you get angry, a rush of adrenaline flows through your body, and it is equal to the rush you got when you were getting high. Like chasing the drug, we start to chase the adrenaline rush, and we start to create chaos with everyone and everything. This is a superficial feeling that hides the truth. The pain, fear, frustration, guilt, and shame are the feelings that anger really covers up.

Anger keeps you sick and away from your true feelings. You can also get a distorted pleasure from anger as though it was a justification to be right and make people, places, and things wrong. When you do this, you take the focus off yourself and tell yourself that it's everyone else's fault. If you want to get angry at something, get angry at your disease.

Take the energy and use it to your benefit. When you feel yourself bubbling up, remove yourself from the situation and call someone like your sponsor or therapist or go to a meeting. Then write down the feelings, how it affected you, what you did about it, what you felt like afterward, and what you need to change.

Anger has always worked against me because I would get out of control. I allowed my anger to control me. Being right was more important then getting my needs met! Boy, do I know how to shortchange myself. Create strategies on how to cope with your anger before it takes control of you.

Anger management is part of a good recovery.

BLAMING

Recovery is a beautiful journey that has its ups and downs. Follow a program of recovery, and you'll enjoy your ups and successfully work through your downs. Blaming others for your misfortunes does nothing for you or your recovery. The only thing you can do is to focus on yourself and change what you need to. Don't waste time trying to change others and prove them wrong; just work on yourself and focus on your recovery.

I promise you, the longer you stay clean, everything will become clear, and you will feel a lot better about yourself and others. Take responsibility for your actions. Do your best to be kind instead of being right. When we take responsibility for our choices, we learn from our mistakes and grow. With a little practice, you'll be amazed. Now get busy and change the things you can.

I refuse to be a puppet on a string. Today I will take responsibility for my own life.

RELATIONSHIPS

Relationships are one of the most difficult situations you will face in recovery. If you're not in one, do your best to stay out of one until you get better acquainted with the new you. Deal with some of your issues: control, anger, jealousy, possessiveness, etc. Now we don't expect you to never feel this way, but through working a program (twelve steps) and seeing a therapist, you will eventually learn to deal with these feelings and not react to them.

Early in recovery, some addicts try to either repair or get into a new relationship. Getting into a new relationship is a disaster early in recovery because you must first work on the relationship with yourself before having a relationship with anyone else. If you are already in a relationship, utilize a therapist to assist you in rebuilding your relationship with your significant other. Be prepared. This may take a long time, or it may not even happen. Please do not put your relationship ahead of your recovery. This is where you have to be a little selfish. Without recovery, there is nothing. If it were meant to be, it would be. Get all the help you can from your sponsor, support group, therapist, psychiatrist, etc.

Many relapses are directly related to people getting into or trying to fix relationships with their significant others. Get your priorities straight. When you learn to love yourself, loving others falls right into place.

There are different types of relationships. Those of you who feel resentments toward your fathers, mothers, sisters, or brothers need to focus on yourselves first. Stop wasting your time trying to change them. Wake up. The only person you can change is you, and you know how difficult that is. There are positive and negative traits in everyone.

Adopt the positive traits and learn from the negative ones. There are no mistakes. Whether you believe it or not, life dealt you the lessons you needed to learn. If you want to play "poor me" or "a victim," go for it! I can tell you that I wasted a lot of years feeling sorry for myself. All I managed to do is go deeper into my addiction and become angrier at my life and others. Learn to live along spiritual lines, and pray for understanding and the gift of being able to forgive. Do the work, and I promise, you will get the job down.

John Giordano

I know that this relationship is the key
to my happiness. Now if I can just find
that door, we'll be home free.

DATING AND GOING OUT

First of all, we need to get our priorities straight. Recovery must come first. In short, do not let going out or hooking up or anything else get in the way of your recovery.

Being addicted to anything takes us away from our path of recovery. Don't hang around places that serve alcohol or drugs or with people who drink or use drugs. It is important not to do anything that would threaten your new lifestyle of being drug- and alcohol-free.

If you do meet someone or are dating someone who is a social drinker, ask them not to drink when they're around you. Please don't act like you can handle it. First of all, there's no need to test yourself. And second, why risk it even if drinking is not your drug of choice? Learn from those who came before you. Being stubborn never really worked for any of us.

SEX AND SEXUAL DESIRE

Hey! Guess what? It's normal to have sexual desires. The only problem is that most addicts equate sex with drugs. IN other words, sex either becomes a drug, or when we have sex, we need drugs. So what is an addict to do? First of all, we need to get our priorities straight. Recovery must come first, in short, do not let lust or anything else get in the way of your recovery.

Being addicted to anything takes us away from our path of recovery. Don't have sex with anyone who drinks or uses drugs or is a danger to your new lifestyle of being drug and alcohol free. If the person is a social drinker, ask them not to drink when they're around. Please don't act like you can handle it. First of all, there's no need to test yourself, and second, why risk it, even if drinking is not your drug of choice? Learn from those who came before you. Being stubborn never really worked for any of us.

MASTURBATION

Just about everybody masturbates, even among people who have sexual relations with a partner. While it once was regarded as a perversion and a sign of a mental problem, masturbation now is regarded as a normal, healthy sexual activity that is pleasant, fulfilling, acceptable, and safe. It is a good way to experience sexual pleasure and can be done throughout life.

Masturbation is only considered a problem when it inhibits sexual activity with a partner, is done in public, or causes significant distress to the person or unmanageability in life. It may cause distress if it is done compulsively or if it interferes with daily life and activities or causes physical problems.

In early recovery especially, the urge to feel better can lead some people to masturbate too much. If you are experiencing distress or unmanageability as a result of either masturbating or the desire to masturbate, talk to your therapist or your sponsor. Don't be too ashamed to reach out for help.

AMENDS

In early recovery, you may want to make amends for the harm you have caused and the people you have hurt, but do not jump the gun. You will start to feel good about yourself and think you can make amends, but take it slow. The steps are in order for a reason.

We are still fragile when we are early in recovery. We may have hurt a lot of people and want to say we are sorry. We think that just because we are sober, people are going to forgive us or accept our apologies—wake up! This is not always going to be the case. When people don't accept our apologies, we get hurt, and we may feel shame or remorse. This can sit in the pit of our stomachs, cause us to eventually get high, and destroy our lives once again.

Amends are measured by what we do and how our behaviors have changed, rather than by what we say. "I'm sorry" gets old after awhile. Do the program the way it is laid out, and the rest will follow. Where there is fear, there is no faith. Without faith, there is no hope.

Good job. Keep reading

TRUST

Some people poke and prod us and continuously ask if we used drugs or alcohol. Do not expect trust right away. Allow people to heal. Some people slip up. When someone goes back to old behaviors or using drugs, they may lose the trust of their peers and any confidence they may have established. The person may lose the belief that they can succeed in recovery. Sometimes you are not quite sure if you can continue without a mood-altering substance, so be patient. Don't play the victim and say to yourself, "No matter what I do, it's never good enough" or "I can't do this." Get out of your self-centeredness and tell yourself you are good enough and you can do it!

You need to realize this is a process, not an event. Change your response, and you change your outcome. As they say in the program, "Give time time!" Don't you just love this saying? Give yourself a break, believe it until it becomes believable, and believe me, it will! Trust in yourself. Eventually, people will too. How long will this take? I don't know. That's up to you and your Higher Power. If so many of us do it, so can you. Remember, no one does it perfectly. So keep going until you get it done.

ASKING FOR HELP

Last but not least, there are those of us who believe we know what we have to do. Unfortunately, asking for help is not part of the plan. There is something you may want to consider. What is the payoff for not asking for help? Using, of course. These types of people help everyone except themselves. They do this because they do not want to take a look at themselves. In most cases, they do not realize that is why they do this. They are the martyrs of addiction, the victims of life. It is okay to help yourself, it is okay to be kind to yourself, and it is okay to love yourself because you can't give away what you don't have.

By asking for help and taking a risk, you learn how to deal with rejection, and you learn to let people help you. You also learn how to be courageous and face your fears. Best of all, you help other people to get out of themselves by helping you. It is all a matter of perception, my friend. Isn't that what life is all about?

CALLING FOR HELP

When feeling low and got no place to turn, call us at (305) 945-8384 or 1-800-559-9503. This is a twenty-four-hours-a-day hotline. We can't keep what we have unless we give it away. If you don't reach out and ask for help because you feel stupid for calling, how can we help you? So don't act stupid. Call if you need to, or at least reach out to someone who understands addiction.

TRIGGERS

Stay away from people, places, and things that trigger your wanting to use or have past memories of using. Hanging around bars or with drinking and drugging friends can and will cause you to relapse. Be careful. Our disease is cunning, baffling, and powerful. It will take us out any way it can. This disease is that fleeting thought or any number of thoughts that take us back to our old ways. It tells us that it was not that bad. Be careful when you get one of these thoughts. Please tell somebody right away. Start telling on your disease! It really makes a difference. We have what is called selective memory. Addicts forget the agony and the shame of using. Don't allow yourself to be fooled one more time. See it for what it really is: death, institutions, jails, as well as loneliness, shame, and guilt. It doesn't have to end this way. It's up to you.

COPING WITH URGES

When you get an urge that doesn't want to go away, consider not pushing it away. Go to another room or safe place and think the urge through. Start with what you would have to do in order to get that drug or drink. Think it all the way until it finally runs out. Remind yourself of what it felt like to run out of the drug and want more. Remember what you had to do to get more and how that made you feel. All that shame and guilt that sat in the pit of your stomach. Remember how you were downright disgusted with yourself, how you hurt yourself, and especially how you hurt the people that really loved you. Whatever it was that initiated your response to destroy yourself one more time was definitely not worth it. So if this ever happens, think it through and immediately call someone safe: a close friend, your sponsor, or your therapist.

Never allow yourself to get hungry, angry, lonely, or tired for any length of time. Get proper rest, six to eight hours a night. Do your best to eat at regular times each day. Don't isolate yourself. When you do, your mind will tend to become a dangerous place to hang out. Before you know it, the using thought has passed. Remember the saying "This too shall pass." And it will.

A NEW LIFE WORTH LIVING

Confused on how to go about living a life of recovery? You are definitely not alone. Many before us had the same concerns. Will I be able to live without drugs and be happy? Can I maintain a recovery lifestyle? Where does my life go from here? So many questions, so few answers. Can I do it? Do I want to do it? (Recovery.) The questions will keep appearing. The good news is that most of your questions will be answered as time goes by.

Learning how to live takes time; being in a hurry will not make it happen any faster. Did you ever stop and think that you are already doing exactly what you need to do? Once you create movement, you then create change. The moment change occurs, opportunity occurs along with all kinds of possibilities. Staying free from drugs or alcohol and risky behaviors creates an environment for healthy progress. Remember: progress, not perfection.

The program of recovery has an abundance of incredibly helpful information, which is based on favorable results: the knowledge of how to live and enjoy life on life's terms. Reach out to those who have come before you. Seek out the winners, the ones with long-time abstinence as well as a lifestyle of recovery. Recovery is not just about drugs and alcohol; it's about spirituality, balance, and finding your purpose in life in order to become all that your Creator intended you to be.

When you seek out the winners of recovery, remember that they are human beings who are struggling with their own character defects. Please don't place them on a pedestal, for you will only become disappointed. Your job is to keep what works for you and discard the rest. Remember that you have choices. Take a risk and ask for help. It may be uncomfortable, but it won't kill you. The consequences of not asking for the help you need can and will be quite severe: death, institutions, jails, and worst of all, living with your shame and guilt until you die. Following these simple suggestions will give you a life beyond your wildest dreams. You see, I know this to be true, I have that life!

DRINK PURE, CLEAN WATER

Approximately 80 percent of the Earth's surface is covered in water. Interestingly, humans are 80 percent water too. Clean, pure water is second only to air in importance. It is important to drink plenty of water in early recovery. Water will help remove the toxins from your body and clean your kidneys and other organs, and it is necessary for all the healing and energy producing systems in the body.

If you can afford a filtration system for your home, go for it. The best systems purify water through two processes: reverse osmosis and microfiltration. Get a system that does both.

If you can't afford a filtration system yet, don't worry. Read the labels on the water you buy and look for those same processes. Avoid water that has not been through a purification system using those methods. Even expensive spring water may not be as purified as the picture on the bottle makes it seem.

Take Your Vitamins

In early recovery, the body needs a lot of nutritional support. Toxins, such as alcohol and drugs, deplete the body of nutrients. Adding to this, the using addict or alcoholic rarely eat well-balanced, healthy meals regularly. Signs of deficiency can range from something as simple as dry chapped lips all the way to hallucinations and other major mental and physical health issues.

These are some of the benefits you can expect from a complete vitamin and mineral supplement:

◊ It assists digestive function.
◊ It boosts brain function.
◊ It gives you added energy.
◊ It helps with weight management and sugar control.
◊ It increases your immune resistance.
◊ It shifts hormonal balances in ways that slow down the process of aging.

It is important to take a multivitamin or multimineral that is easy for the body to absorb and use. For this reason, many experts believe that capsules containing a loose powder form, or even drinks, are better than hard tablets. Multivitamins are best taken with food and during the daytime. Amino acids need to be taken on an empty stomach forty-five minutes before eating or two hours after eating; otherwise, they don't work well.

FELLOWSHIPPING

Fellowshipping is about making new friends in recovery and developing a positive support group. When we used, we had a support group that helped us find ways and means. In recovery, we want a support group that will help us learn a new positive, healthy way to live.

Going to meetings is very important. Just as important are the meeting before the meeting and the meeting after the meeting. In early recovery especially, it is important to make new friends with common interests—like staying clean. There are many ways to fellowship with the people that you meet at meetings. Going for coffee or dinner after the meeting with others from the meeting is a good way to make new friends and develop a support group. Some areas also have picnics and dances and local conventions.

You don't have to like everyone you meet at the meetings. Just get to know a few people and remember to stick with the winners. Those people who go to meetings work the steps and help others.

Go Organic

Basically, organic foods are produced using all natural methods. Technically, these are foods that are produced using methods that do not involve modern synthetic inputs, do not contain genetically modified organisms, and are not processed using irradiation, industrial solvents, or chemical food additives.

During active addiction, we pollute our bodies with many chemicals and substances even beyond what we used. For example, some drugs are processed using chemicals that are even more harmful than the drug itself.

In early recovery, do your best to buy all-natural foods. Even the large grocery store chains have organic sections now. The fewer chemicals we introduce into the body, the faster we can heal.

TAKE A WALK

Walking is great exercise, and it improves mood too! It's a great way to have a conversation with someone too because sometimes we have difficulty looking someone in the eye and telling them how we really feel or what we are going through. Walking becomes a way to talk without being confrontational or fearful.

Early in recovery, it is hard to focus and stay still enough to meditate. Walking meditations are a good way to get started. Remember the saying "Stop and smell the flowers." Become aware of the beauty around you. It's there you just have to look for it.

TREATMENT MODALITIES AND THERAPIES

Each of the therapies and modalities described in the following section are actually in use at our holistic center in North Miami Beach, Florida. We have conducted research with leading scientists from around the world to determine the impact of each of the modalities. Our research has provided the evidence needed to know that these modalities work. This is why we call our techniques and our program evidence based.

The research we have conducted is available through a number of resources. You can begin by going to www.holisticaddictioninfo.com or searching for our articles online. A list of our publications is included in the section "Bibliography and Suggested Readings" of this book.

If you would like more in-depth information about these modalities, we offer courses taught by some of the world's leading scientists and professors through the National Institute for Holistic Addiction Studies. The mission of NIFHAS is to integrate wisdom pathways with advances in traditional and holistic medicine in order to gain a broader understanding of addictions and co-occurring disorders and to develop effective, evidence-based, holistic addiction treatment modalities based on valid and reliable research. NIFHAS offers continuing education certification and individual courses to students all over the world through an online learning environment available twenty-four hours a day with the flexibility to take courses when and where your schedule permits. Visit NIFHAS and learn more at www.nifhas.com.

Also, most of the products that are discussed in this book can be purchased through our holistic center at www.holisticaddictioninfo.com.

Remember, information is power. This section of the book was developed to give you the power to create a plan that will help you achieve lasting recovery.

THERAPY

Go to a therapist that is familiar with addiction and dual disorders. Having a dual disorder means that both the disease of addiction and a possible mental disorder or chemical imbalance are present. Examples of these mental disorders or chemical imbalances are bipolar disorder, obsessive-compulsive disorder, attention deficit disorder, schizophrenia, and depression, among others.

Heavy metal toxicity and nutrient deficiencies can also cause the same symptoms associated with the abovementioned disorders as well as others.

Definitions of the most common mental disorders associated with addiction are available in the appendices at the back of this book followed by the glossary.

> **Going to therapy does not mean you are damaged or crazy or broken. Most people in therapy are everyday, ordinary people with everyday human problems. If you are afraid of being judged for going to therapy, it is probably your own inner critic judging you. Therapy would be a way to build self-esteems and free yourself from the opinions of others.**
>
> From http://www.goodtherapy.org

Ideally, you want to look for a therapist that understands addiction from a nutritional and dual diagnosis perspective. Many addicts and alcoholics, once clean, work in the field of addiction recovery. Make sure the type of therapist that you go to helps you to build up your positive attributes and does not come from a shaming place. This is important because in the beginning, as you get clean, you may become painfully aware of many things that you did or that were done to you during your active addiction.

Find a therapist who knows addiction, who is trained in neurolinguistic programming, who knows Gestalt therapy, and who believes in a humanistic approach.

It is important for a therapist to be a good listener, but there is more to a good therapist. A good therapist should be compassionate, empathetic, and genuine. You will feel their warmth, and you feel comfortable with them. You want a therapist who is dynamic and alive and who gives you specific feedback even in the beginning. Overall, a good therapist match for you is someone who is open-minded and leaves you feeling good about yourself and hopeful about your future.

EVALUATIONS AND TESTING

Evaluation is a key part of your treatment and recovery experience. Would you allow a surgeon to operate on you after only a few questions? The same is true for your recovery. Each individual is a reflection of a very personal and unique combination of the past, present, and future, their thoughts, feelings, their body, its systems and performance, as well as that unnameable part in each of us that we refer to as the spirit. In order to create real and lasting change, we need to take a comprehensive—*holistic*—inventory of ourselves.

Your therapist or your doctor may ask you to participate in a psychiatric evaluation. This is one way for them to be able to identify and determine treatments that will help you. Don't be ashamed if the result is that your doctor asks you to be on medication. Many of us have a chemical imbalance and need to be evened out. Especially in the beginning, many of us need help to stabilize our emotions and feelings. Most addicts with chronic relapses have an underlying disorder that is quite often never addressed. It is helpful if your psychiatrist has experience or training with addiction and is familiar with the use of therapies and treatments described in this book such as nutraceuticals, amino acid therapy, and other complementary medical treatments such as acupuncture.

There are other ways for your doctor or therapist to evaluate you as well. We suggest that you get a physical examination and blood and urine tests. Be sure to have your doctor check for hyper or hypoglycemia and *Candida albicans* infection, which can cause irritability, depression, and confused thinking. You may also want to get tested for heavy metal toxicity and nutrient deficiencies. Some forms of metal toxicity and nutrient deficiencies can imitate the symptoms of mental health disorders. There are resources in the end of this book to help you get tested.

In her book *The Mood Cure*, Julia Ross has a four-part mood type questionnaire that is designed to identify your false mood symptoms, or those symptoms that are caused by factors other than your real feelings. She and many others in the field of treating addiction believe that often there is a brain chemistry issue that can be resolved with nutritional support. The idea is that once you have identified and treated those symptoms, which are the result of these brain chemistry issues, the psychotherapy, twelve-step meetings and other resources that you are using to overcome addiction, will be more effective.

Toward the end of this book, after the glossary section, is a relapse prevention questionnaire. Part of the questionnaire deals with identifying symptoms that may be a result of poor diet, lack of sleep, or brain chemistry issues. It also has suggested remedies for different symptoms.

RECOVERING STRATEGY

Having a good recovery strategy starts with a plan. People who are effective at achieving their goals begin with a plan. In recovery, we do the same, and it starts with a daily plan. A plan is really just a list of things you feel you have to do to achieve a goal.

We suggest that you purchase a day planner book, and each day ask yourself, "What do I need to do today to stay clean?" Those are the first and most important things that you will write on your daily plan. We call this your *intention*.

When you were drinking and drugging, you probably ignored your responsibilities. While you cannot turn back the hands of time, you can begin to assume the responsibilities of daily life now. Include those things that you will do today to resume normal responsibilities of school, work, and family on your daily plan.

Getting Clean and Learning to Live

When I was 18 I began to live on the streets. I come from a very upper class family. Suddenly, I did not have a home, I did not eat or wash regularly – I lost all my living skills. By the time that I got to treatment center number 17, I did not know how to do the things that regular people do as part of their regular day. I was even like a child who did not want to take his bath sometimes. Everything had to be planned – washing myself, my clothes, learning to prepare meals and remembering to eat; even scheduling bedtime. I remember when I first started to use a daily planner. I had to put planning my day on the plan for the day! And now, I have almost a whole year clean. Building the daily planner into my recovery strategy taught me how to set goals for myself and take care of myself. I was able to approach my day one step at a time and I continue to achieve my goals the same way.

Michael H, Recovering Alcoholic and Addict

Although we cannot turn back time, there are some things we may need to do that are left over from the past. Make a list of these things, but be careful. Sometimes it seems we have fallen so far behind on everything from school, to work, to bills, and more that we will never catch up. It is important not to become overwhelmed, so look at each item on your list and prioritize them. Consider this list your long-term goals.

That way you can chip away at them over time without feeling overwhelmed or anxious. Talk to your therapist, your sponsor, or any other person whom you respect and trust. Make sure they understand addiction and let them help you with your decision making. Keep in mind that your brain only seems to be working properly and that the person you are seeking guidance from needs to understand addiction in order to effectively help you. There is no shame in asking for help, so get rid of the excuses. Recovery comes before anything or anyone. If you put anyone or anything before your recovery, you are sure to use and lose—no recovery, no hope, and no life worth living.

John Giordano

MENTAL HEALTH AND MEDICATION

Anyone can develop a mental illness. Some disorders are mild, short-term, or temporary, and there are others that are more severe and long lasting. Having a mental health disorder is not a sign of weakness. It is just like having a cold or other illness. And often, medications are used to manage the symptoms of the disorder. Medications do not *cure* mental health disorders, but they can often relieve some of the discomfort and difficulty coping associated with the disorder.

Sometimes the symptoms or the disorders are temporary and may be a direct result of using. This can happen due to the damage we do to our brains when we use. Even when this is the case, it is very important that you take the disorder and the doctor's recommendations seriously. Addiction and alcoholism are life-threatening diseases, just like cancer and other medical diseases. If your symptoms are a consequence of using, they are not any less real or painful. Give yourself a break and seek professional help in managing your symptoms.

If you need to be on medication, it may take from four to six weeks to stabilize. If you feel sluggish and out of sorts, call your doctor. Most often, it's your body adjusting to the medication. After four to six weeks, if you still don't feel right, speak to your doctor again. Everyone is different. Be patient. Sometimes you may have to change your medication a few times. Don't get discouraged. If you need medication and don't take it, the alternative will be a never-ending story.

Some medications do have side effects. Every time that you receive a prescription from the pharmacy, there is an insert that explains the dosage instructions and the possible side effects. Dr. Hyla Cass, prominent holistic medical doctor, has a great book that you can use as a resource to help you prevent and manage the side effects of many medications. Her book is called *Supplement Your Prescription*. (Details for ordering are in the recommended reading section.)

After you have been taking your medication and start feeling good, please don't stop or adjust your dosage without the supervision of your doctor. This is a very common mistake for people to make, and generally if they do, they relapse right after. If by any chance you consider this, call your doctor.

If you are leery of taking medication, talk to your doctor. There are many alternative treatments available and indicated for use for a variety of mental health disorders. Many of the symptoms of mental health disorders can be relieved effectively and sometimes more safely with nutraceuticals and other alternative and complementary treatments such as those discussed in this book. Similarly, there are herbs that are used for relaxation, and there are herbs that will help with depression. You will find a series of short questionnaires at the end of this book that could help you begin a nutraceuticals program. It is important, however, to involve your doctor. Do not try to diagnose and treat yourself. Don't shortchange yourself. Give it a chance.

NATIONAL INSTITUTE FOR MENTAL HEALTH RECOMMENDATIONS REGARDING MENTAL HEALTH MEDICATIONS:

When you go to the doctor, be sure to take a list of your medications with you – include medications, over-the-counter drugs, vitamins, supplements, and even herbal teas.

When you are prescribed medications for any reason, the National Institute of Mental Health recommends that you ask the following questions:

- What is the name of the medication, and what is it supposed to do?
- How and when do I take it, and when do I stop taking it?
- What foods, drinks, or other medications should I avoid while taking the prescribed medication?
- Should it be taken with food or on an empty stomach?
- Is it safe to drink alcohol while on this medication?
- What are the side effects, and what should I do if they occur?
- Is a Patient Package Insert for the medication available?

http://www.nimh.nih.gov/health/publications/medications/complete-index.shtml

Learn to work with the professionals who are treating you. *Allow them to do their job.* Part of your job, however, is to learn all you can about the medications that you are taking. This includes any prescribed medications, over-the-counter medications, nutraceuticals, and herbal supplements. There are many resources available today, especially on the Internet.

I'm having difficulty finding my way. I need to reach out for help. What happened to my pink cloud?

VITAMIN THERAPY AND NUTRACEUTICALS

Nutraceutical therapy is extremely important. There is a great deal of research on the importance of proper nutrition. Dr. Stephen Schoenthaler, University of California professor and Linus Pauling Award winner, conducted studies that show that adding a nutritional supplement to the diet can decrease violence or acting-out behaviors and increase IQ.

There is an emerging field of medicine called orthomolecular medicine, which is having a strong, positive impact in addiction and mental health treatment. Orthomolecular medicine has its origins in the concept of "making whole" or returning the body to its natural state of wellness. One of the ways to do this is through the use of vitamin therapies and nutraceuticals.

Vitamin therapy and nutraceuticals refer to the use of specific foods, food ingredients, or dietary supplements to support, enhance, or develop a state of healthy functioning of one or more of the body's systems. Vitamin therapy and nutraceuticals make available the ingredients and the environment for the body to return to its natural state of well-being.

> *Without the nutraceutical therapy, I would never have been able to sit still long enough to get anything from group or meetings. One thing that is really cool is that when I am feeling anxious, there is actually a nutraceutical to help me with my anxiety. It's not like taking a pill because I know that the product is all natural and it is helping my body to heal and helping my brain to remember how to relax by itself.*
>
> *There is also a sleep formula that helped me relax enough, and turn the constant thinking off for long enough, to finally get some rest. And when I wake up in the morning, there is no hangover or dull feeling. I wake up refreshed and rested. The vitamin therapy and nutraceuticals were an important part of treatment that I didn't get anywhere else. I think they made a huge difference for me.*
>
> *Because I wasn't so filled with anxiety and run-away thoughts, I was able to pay attention in group and at the meetings.*
>
> Gina, Recovering Addict

Recovery is an ongoing practice; it is not something we do for a little while. Our disease is a chronic progressive illness that can be arrested if we follow a recovery lifestyle. Always check with your doctor before taking these vitamins and herbs.

When you first get clean, we recommend that you begin a mild detoxification and nutrient replacement program. Your focus should begin with detoxifying and refortifying the liver. Simultaneously, you will want to replace nutrients that were depleted during the period of using and add a supplement to support brain healing and function.

We also suggest that you add a probiotic product into your supplementation program. During active addiction, we disturb the natural flora of the intestines. The intestinal flora is important because they help digest and absorb the nutrients in food and vitamins. Probiotics and enzymes are a way to replace and replenish the natural flora of your body.

The number and type of supplements available can be quite overwhelming. For this reason, we have developed a recommended product line. We have been using these products successfully with clients for several years. It has taken years to develop balanced formulations that will help create a sense of well-being and assist greatly in reducing cravings. Years of experience have demonstrated that these products help to rebuild and restore healthy functioning and reverse the damage caused by drugs and alcohol.

> **Holistic Multi Vitamin and Mineral** This formula is designed to help balance the nervous system and strengthen the whole body.
>
> **Holistic Anti-Anxiety/Sleep Formulation** This formula is designed to assist in creating a normal sleep pattern and calm the nervous system
>
> **Holistic Mental Clarity Formulation** This formula is designed to help the body, clear the mind, enhance thinking, and restore a healthy energy level.
>
> **Liver Self Defense and Companion (Hep C Duo)** This formula is designed to help significantly strengthen the liver and create more energy.
>
> To order any of the vitamins described above, call John Giordano 786-271-5732 holisticaddictioninfo.com.

There are also products that are specific to the substances you used and symptoms that you are experiencing. In the questionnaire toward the end of this book is a section to help you determine additional needs. There are also suggested readings and books to help guide you to find the products best suited for you during each phase of your recovery.

We also recommend that you drink the mental clarity protein drink every morning. Most addicts are protein deficient. Use other herbs and vitamins as directed. Don't expect an immediate response. These are not drugs, but these are ways of helping rebuild what we have destroyed: our mind, body, and spirit.

> *SUGGGESTION: every 30 to 45 days, stop all supplements for three days; then begin again where you left off. This will help your body better utilize the supplements.*

DIET

1. Diet is very important, especially early in the recovery process. Here are some suggestions to guide you:

2. Do your best not to eat white flour products or products with processed sugar, such as bread, cakes, cookies, and donuts, which have both. Food allergies and addictions are associated with these foods, and after the initial "rush," eating these types of foods can lead to craving more and feeling irritable. These foods can also cause headaches, constipation, and sinus trouble.

3. Do your best not to eat dairy products such as cheese, milk, ice cream, and yogurt. While these foods do have some nutritional value, many adults develop intolerance to dairy, and eating it can lead to stomach and intestinal discomfort, gas, increased mucus production, and other allergy symptoms.

4. Beware of caffeine products such as coffee, tea, colas, and *especially energy drinks*. Many of these products have a great deal of sugar as well. In early recovery especially, our body is fatigued. The systems in our body, such as the adrenals and the kidneys and thyroid, which help produce the energy responses naturally, have already been stressed out. To artificially stimulate these systems

with caffeine and energy drinks will cause further damage. Besides the "crash" after the product wears off, it will now be harder and will take longer for the natural systems to heal. These products can lead to feelings of fatigue, irritability, bipolar disorder-like symptoms, and even to misdiagnosis of a psychological disorder.

5. Drink plenty of unsweetened juice and lots of water (about three quarts, or about six bottles, of water a day). Everything that happens in the body—all the healing, every process from digestion to thought, every action—requires the presence of water. Drinking plenty of water will allow you to support the detoxification process as well as the healing processes going on in your body during early recovery.

6. Eat five small meals a day. This will help to keep your energy level up and may help speed up your metabolism. Complex carbohydrates (baked potatoes, vegetables) are good forms of energy. Eat fruit and cereal in the morning. Eat a lot of greens and protein dishes (five to six ounces of fish, chicken, tofu, etc.) throughout the day, and eat small portions of carbohydrates for dinner, such as sweet potatoes or vegetables.

7. Get proteins into your diet. Fish, turkey, chicken, legumes, and soy products are

good sources of proteins. Avoid tuna and swordfish as they have been shown to have high levels of toxins, including mercury. Try to find free-range chicken in your local markets.

8. Go organic. Organic foods are produced without synthetic or unnatural inputs, like chemical pesticides or fertilizers. Organic foods do not contain genetic modifications and are not processed using irradiation, industrial solvents, or chemical food additives. Most major food stores have organic food departments in the produce section, the butcher section, and packaged foods.

Eating poorly or eating high-sugar and high-fat foods can stimulate the craving centers in the brain and may ultimately create a negative attitude or frustration. No one is perfect, so give yourself a break. Do your best to change the way you eat. You will find that when you eat well, you can produce a healthier outlook, feel good about yourself, see things positively, and slowly create change in yourself for the better.

Note on Eating Disorders

Many professionals and doctors believe that there is a relationship between eating disorders and addiction. There is a growing understanding that eating disorders and substance abuse/alcoholism often co-occur, especially in females. In fact, females who have been diagnosed with either a substance abuse disorder or an eating disorder are upto five times more likely to also have the other disorder than women in the general population.

Some even propose that eating disorders are a form of addiction. What we know for sure is that certain eating behaviors, such as strong diet restrictions, starving yourself, throwing up and extreme over-exercising can stimulate the reward pathways in your brain, just like when we use.

As well, many people noticed that with certain drugs, not only did they feel good, but they were able to loose weight easily. For some, this may have been the catalyst that caused the drug abuse that eventually resulted in addiction.

Whether your substance abuse was associated with an eating disorder or not, if you are vomiting, binging-purging, restricting or over-exercising, you can seriously harm yourself. These behaviors can lead to heart attack, stroke and other serious conditions, and may also make relapse more likely.

For this reason we suggest that if you have been involved in any of the noted behaviors, (like vomiting, binging, purging, restricting, over-exercising, or starving) or are having any difficulty managing your weight or adjusting to a new body image, *please* seek professional help.

EXERCISE

Exercise is an important part of any recovery program. The physical benefits of exercise include improved heart and lung functioning, improved strength and stamina, weight management, and more.

Aerobic exercise, such as walking, jogging, bike riding, or swimming causes our body to produce natural chemicals that relieve pain and reduce anxiety, depression, and stress.

Exercise is also a social activity. Going to the gym or getting involved with a team or group of people to exercise regularly can prevent isolating. Exercise also provides some time where you are not thinking about your problems.

People who exercise regularly are also more likely to sleep better and feel more refreshed upon waking.

Exercise also increases the blood flow to the brain, transporting extra oxygen and nutrients to help the brain heal.

I have always enjoyed exercising. You could say that exercising and athletics are 'what I know'. During treatment I was able to get back into the gym for a long time. I have several years clean now and I still work out everyday.

At first, going to the gym was something to do. It kept me busy and it kept me from gaining too much weight in the beginning of my recovery.

Now, walking on the treadmill is my anti-stress therapy. It helps me wind down at the end of the day. It gives me time to do some reading. It keeps me from isolating and helps me meet new people. It also supports my health and fitness goals.

Shea H, Recovering Alcoholic and Addict

Remember to get your doctor's permission and recommendations, especially if you have any underlying health problems, like high blood pressure, diabetes, or heart disease.

Once you receive medical clearance to begin an exercise program, begin with walking at a moderate pace for ten to fifteen minutes a day. Then increase the duration slowly to thirty to forty-five minutes a day. Swimming is also great way to get in shape.

When working out, make sure your heartbeat is up and your breathing is hard. A good way to make sure that you are not overdoing it is to try to speak while you are exercising. You should be able to have a short conversation during aerobic exercise.

Weight lifting is good when combined with aerobic exercise. Weight lifting will help you rebuild muscle and tone your body as well. If you are going to weight lift, always have a workout buddy for safety. You may want to work with a trainer, at least at first, to learn how to do the exercises safely and effectively.

Team and partner sports are a great way to meet new people and stay in shape. Tennis, basketball, and volleyball can be used in an aerobic fitness plan. In winter months especially, many malls have morning walking clubs. Summertime offers bicycling clubs and beach sports as well.

MEDITATION AND SOUND TECHNOLOGIES

We use recordings with music under meditations at our center to relieve anxiety and support a relaxed and open state in our clients and staff. Some of the recordings are subliminal—the sound of the recording cannot be heard because it is buried deep under the music. This type of recording will have an impact even if you don't actually hear it. Another type of technology we use is binaural, which means that it is recorded with two separate microphones and intended for headphones. There is research demonstrating the beneficial effects of these modalities on PTSD and other stress disorders, generalized anxiety, insomnia, and sleep disturbances as well as the stress-associated health problems such as high blood pressure, headaches, and fatigue.

The binaural technologies work by inducing different brain wave frequencies. Before group therapy, we stimulate an alpha state, which is associated with superlearning ability, relaxed focus, access to the subconscious, and spiritual awareness.

We find that clients are less likely to act out negatively during group therapy, less confrontational in general, and more open to suggestions when using this technology.

Music has played an important role in our lives as individuals and as a race because it has physical and psychological/emotional impacts on us. For this reason, we know that music can also have a therapeutic effect. Therapeutic music and binaural audio tones are very effective ways to promote relaxation and stress management skills.

We combine this technology with guided meditation to achieve a deeper level of action. We also use an enhanced healing version of this technology to support the development of self-esteem and to change negative thinking patterns.

These technologies have proven invaluable in pain management. The body responds to pain with a stress response, which can actually worsen the pain. Using the guided meditations and sound technologies, clients are able to activate different levels of consciousness and awareness. The focus is moved away from the pain response to a more comfortable level of awareness.

For more information and to purchase these technologies, contact the John Giordano 786-271-5732 holisticaddictioninfo.com.

When I was 9 years old, I began having really bad headaches. They were diagnosed as migraines and I was given pain medication for them.

By 23 I was married and I was pregnant and so hopeful about the future. Something went wrong and she was still-born. I was given pain medication for the c-section and at her funeral I never cried – I felt nothing I was so doped up. A few years later I was diagnosed with Lupus. Again, legitimate pain pills for my legitimate pain.

Something that really helped me during treatment and even to this day, almost 4 years later, are the music and meditation downloads that began using in treatment. I use this technology every day. I find that listening to the meditation or the subliminal recordings helps me stay centered and relaxed through out my day. This technology has helped me discover a peace and serenity that I never thought possible.

I have been able to learn alternative ways to manage the pain of Lupus. Learning how to relax and using the guided meditations has helped tremendously. Honestly, I don't have pain like I did when I was using. I feel good and I feel good about myself.

Marcy U, Recovering Addict

MASSAGE

Most people associate massage with a life of luxury: cruise ships, spas, and vacations. The truth, however, is that various massage treatments have been used for centuries because of their health and medical benefits. Massage is used in traditional medicine by physical therapists, occupational therapists, and orthopedic specialties.

During massage, your body's muscles, skin, and tendons are manipulated, relieving tension and releasing toxins. Massage calms the nervous system and promotes a sense of relaxation and well-being, reducing tension and anxiety. The physical action of massage improves the circulation of blood and lymph, which allows more nutrients and oxygen to be delivered to where they are needed most. Similarly, massage supports the elimination of the waste products and other toxins in your body.

Massage is also an effective tool in managing chronic pain in conditions such as arthritis, sciatica, fibromyalgia, and general muscle pain.

Research has demonstrated that massage is helpful in these and other conditions:

◊ *Anxiety*. Massage reduced anxiety in depressed children and anorexic women. It also reduced anxiety and withdrawal symptoms in adults trying to quit smoking. It was found to reduce anxiety in psychiatric patients as well .

◊ *Pain*. Pain was decreased in people with fibromyalgia, arthritis, migraines, and recent surgery. Back pain also might be relieved by massage.

◊ *Sports-related soreness*. Some athletes receive massages after exercise, especially to the muscles they use most in their sport or activity. A massage might help increase blood flow to your muscles and may reduce muscle soreness after you exercise.

◊ *Alcohol withdrawal*. Massage during withdrawal from alcohol has shown benefits when combined with traditional medical treatment by increasing feelings of support, safety, and engagement in the therapy.

◊ *Immune system benefits*. For people with HIV who participated in massage, studies showed an increased number of natural killer cells, which are thought to defend the body from viral and cancer cells. The action of massage stimulates the lymphatic system and your body's filtering system as well.

◊ *Cancer treatment.* People with cancer who received regularly scheduled massage therapy during treatment reported less anxiety, pain, and fatigue.

◊ *Self-esteem.* Because massage involves direct contact with another person through touch, it can make you feel cared for. That special attention can improve self-image in people with physical disabilities and terminal illnesses. And using touch to convey caring can help children with severe physical disabilities.

For the first year, do your best to get at least one deep tissue massage a week. This massage will help in relieving emotional stress, which is trapped in the very fibers of your muscles. Our bodies get stressed, not just our minds. Learn to treat all three areas: body, mind, and spirit. Massage will help you to stay centered and relaxed. It is another way to get high—high on life! If you don't have the money to get a professional massage, trade off with a friend.

NATURAL DETOXIFICATION AND SPA TREATMENTS

Current medical drug and alcohol detoxification facilities, known commonly as detox, serve primarily as stabilization units. Their purpose is to manage the acute withdrawal symptoms.

These facilities offer the patient the opportunity to stop using for a short period of time and generally provide medications to manage the symptoms associated with drug and alcohol withdrawals. The most important role they play is in monitoring the medical health and safety of the patient during the critical immediate withdrawal especially from substances known to have high-risk withdrawal symptoms such as seizures and inflated blood pressure.

Using current detox methods, failure occurs much more often than not, and most people never make it to receive the type of treatment they need. This is because most of the individuals leaving detoxification centers are still drug affected, rendering them unable to make clear decisions about treatment programs and recovery options. In order to effectively combat this alarming and growing problem, alternative treatment methods must be explored. These should be used in conjunction with other therapies.

Proper diet and nutrition consisting of vitamin C, amino acids, essential fatty acids, and proteins can have a very positive effect. Vitamin C is a very potent antioxidant and will help cleanse and destroy free radicals in the tissues. It also aids in releasing intestinal toxins, which are an important component of getting clean and sober.

I suggest taking 3,000 mg of vitamin C every four hours for three to five days. Amino acids, especially glutamine, will stimulate the body's natural opiates and endorphins to help alleviate some cravings. Essential fatty acids, such as flax oil, in combination with foods containing proteins (cysteine of methionine), such as yogurt, eggs, codfish, sesame paste, garlic, and onions, will allow fat-soluble toxins to become water for excretion through sweat and urine.

In order to facilitate and expedite excretion of toxic substance, perspiration must be enhanced. This should be done through exercise and steam therapy, such as Turkish steam baths, infrared, or a hot whirlpool bath. Outdoor activities like beach outings are also good. Following heavy perspiration, the individual should clean themselves with a high-fat soap to remove toxins excreted on the surface of the skin and prevent their reabsorption.

Another area to consider when approaching detoxification from alcohol and drugs is the colon. The colon is a major part of the excretory system and is responsible for eliminating food and other body wastes as well as protecting us from infection and disease. In a normally functioning colon, cleansing is achieved with the help of billions of friendly bacteria that make up some 70 percent of the dry weight of our fecal waste.

The delicate balance of this internal ecosystem can very easily be disturbed by factors including stress, pollution, poor food and drink choices, certain drugs, smoking, and exposure to toxic substances. A series of three colonics given in a one-week period, beginning about the third or fourth day of detox treatment, will remove the waste products and toxins created by years of mistreating your body and will definitely aid in your intestine's ability to absorb nutrients. You only have one body, so treat it with love and care.

Hyperbaric oxygen therapy has been used by Russains for over twenty years to help with detox. Also, Dr. Ken Blums formula SynaptaGenX and John Giordano's formulation are also very beneficial.

ACUPUNCTURE

Acupuncture dates back thousands of years. Specifically, acupuncture is six thousand years old and ear acupuncture is 2,500 years old. The purpose of acupuncture is to restore balance in the bodies energy system called chi. Basically, chi, or life energy, is believed to flow along pathways throughout the body (called meridians). When there is a blockage of the energy flow, an excess of energy builds up on one side of the blockage and a deficiency is created on the other. These blockages in energy correlate with pain and disease states. Acupuncture corrects the excesses and deficiencies of chi along the meridians, restoring the body's ability to achieve balance and wellness. This may be accomplished using needles or electrical stimuli.

Today, acupuncture is practiced internationally. Its practitioners include professional acupuncturists and a variety of other health care providers including medical doctors. More than two thousand acupuncture points are now recognized by licensed acupuncturists.

Acupuncture has been used successfully on one point in the ear to relieve opiate withdrawal symptoms and was first used as part of a methadone program Bronx, New York. Over several years, the detox protocol was eventually refined and is now offered through providers who are trained by the National Acupuncture Detoxification Association (NADA). For the past thirty-five years, the use of acupuncture detox in a wide variety of clinical settings including county jails, maximum-security prisons, outpatient drug treatment programs, homeless shelters, and mental health facilities has been studied with overall positive results in many cases.

According to the literature, acupuncture can help with urges and cravings and will help your brain and body heal. Specifically, it helps replenish and repair chemical systems in the brain that we deplete when we use drugs and alcohol. Acupuncture is not a cure for addiction, but it is a powerful piece of the recovery puzzle.

MILD HYPERBARIC OXYGEN
THERAPY

Hyperbaric oxygen therapy (HBOT) can be used to help repair and restore the body and mind. Not too long ago, doctors and scientists thought that once damaged, tissue in the brain could not heal. Recently doctors using hyperbaric oxygen therapy (HBOT) have demonstrated that not only can brain tissue heal, even brain tissue with old injuries can be restored to functioning. HBOT is used in addiction treatment to reverse the damage done when abusing alcohol and drugs.

HBOT is a method of administering increased levels of oxygen at greater atmospheric pressure in order to help heal tissue damage. HBOT is effective at restoring cell function to tissue everywhere in the body, including the brain. By providing increased oxygen levels in a pressurized chamber, we are able to deliver higher concentrations of oxygen than what the brain normally receives through breathing. Some of its effects are to promote the growth of new blood vessels, to decrease swelling and inflammation, to deactivate and promote the release of toxins, and to promote overall healing.

HBOT was first used to treat "the bends," which is a condition caused when scuba divers ascend too rapidly from deep in the ocean. It is now widely used for a variety of other conditions.

Advantages of HBOT include that it is cost-effective, noninvasive, safe, and works well with other treatments.

HBOT is an accepted, reimbursable treatment for more than fifteen different types of disorders ranging from carbon monoxide poisoning to crush injuries of the brain to diabetic wounds. HBOT is also used for many other conditions where it may or may not be reimbursable.

The use of HBOT in stroke victims and in other victims of brain injuries provides a foundation for efficacy with use to treat the brain injuries that result from long-term drug and alcohol abuse. Brain scans of addicts show areas of reduced circulation and functioning in the brain, much like those of stroke and gas poisoning victims. The ability of HBOT to restore the cellular functioning of damaged tissues in the brain has been demonstrated in stroke victims both immediately following the tissue damage as well as much later.

We have used HBOT at our treatment center with excellent success. Usually, HBOT is packaged in bundles of twenty sessions, about an hour and half each, to support lasting change. However, clients claim that they feel the difference after as few as three sessions.

We recommend combining the use of the HBOT with the Hep C Companion formulation nutraceuticals or another nutraceuticals protocol, which includes antioxidants to eliminate the free radicals associated with the use of high levels of oxygen.

We also suggest the use of a relaxation or meditation CD during HBOT treatment. Although it cannot be worn inside the chamber for safety reasons, a compact disc player can be set up so that the contents are heard inside the chamber. It is very relaxing and can help reduce some of the initial fear clients may experience when first using the chamber.

If you think of the brain as fertile soil in which the flower of life grows, HBOT is the sunshine and nutraceuticals are the rain.

I came to G & G Holistic after multiple treatment episodes at other treatment centers. I had a history of methamphetamine abuse, hepatitis C and was diagnosed as a bi-polar. At intake I remember that I actually told the therapist that this was probably my last chance. At that time, I was unemployed and unemployable, had no real friends and no place to live.

I was one of the first people to use the Hyperbaric therapy regularly. I have a standing appointment pretty much everyday. My ability to think and make decisions has improved beyond what I ever imagined. When I came to treatment, I was diagnosed as having bi-polar disorder as well. The use of the hyperbaric chamber and the nutraceuticals that I take as part of the hyperbaric therapy has helped to moderate my bi-polar. I still take medications for bi-polar. I probably always will. But now that I have been using the hyperbarics, I think they can actually work better.I know that I am working better.

Isaac M., Recovering Addict

HARMONIAL COLOR/SOUND/ IMAGERY THERAPY ENHANCEMENT

Harmonial is a therapy developed in France. It is used to relieve anxiety, panic attacks, post-traumatic stress disorder (PTSD), and sleep disorders. We have also found it to be effective in relieving symptoms of addiction withdrawal. The therapy is based on the effects that different colors, visualizations, sounds, and smells have on feelings and mood.

The contents of each session are individualized to the client and his/her mood and stress level. Harmonial therapy uses color, images, sounds, and music to put the client into a deep state of relaxation. During this deep state of relaxation, issues that are causing stress are able to surface. Sometimes you will have a dream about the issue or you may find yourself remembering something you had forgotten. These issues are now ready to be processed safely with your therapist or counselor.

We have added the element of aromatherapy with essential oils because essential oils have historically been shown to calm and relax emotions as well as enhance focus, attention, and memory. It immediately goes to the brain and tells your body how to react. Different oils will help to relax or stimulate. This message is then sent to the rest of the body via the nervous system.

There are no known side effects of harmonial therapy. Occasionally, you may have strong emotions after a session. It is safe for use with conventional medicine as well. At least ten sessions are recommended for maximum benefit, but the number can vary based on the issues being addressed and the individual.

> *In the field of addiction, Harmonial Therapy is a bright light at the end of a very long, dark tunnel. It accomplishes the goal every alcoholic and drug addict would like to achieve – A Natural High.*
>
> Jack Kelly, Certified Addiction Professional

NLP: Goal Setting and Self-Esteem Building

Many people self-sabotage. We all have a self-limiting belief: a belief about ourselves that has been stopping us from achieving our goals and enjoying our life. Self-limiting beliefs are often painful to acknowledge, and the use of drugs and alcohol is a way to ignore or numb the pain that comes from this belief.

This requires that we change the way we speak about ourselves. This happens both internally, through self-talk and thinking, as well as externally, speaking to others differently. We begin to act differently, and this boosts our self-esteem.

We use NLP techniques to help build goals. Every Monday, choose a reasonable and achievable goal from the recovery strategy that you have built. Write the goal as your intention for the week and then write down the activities that you will perform to achieve the goal. Include naming a person that will help you be responsible for your goal, like a sponsor or someone else you trust.

As the week progresses, think about what it will be like to achieve the goal and revisit that feeling often. Remember to praise yourself when you complete activities that put you closer to the goal.

Building self-esteem requires that we do things differently, like setting and achieving reasonable goals. Practicing positive self-talk, being patient with yourself, and acknowledging yourself are important parts of building self-esteem.

There are group and solo exercises that you can perform to improve your self-talk and your self-esteem. We offer clients a ropes course to build self-esteem and to learn how to trust themselves and others. We also use recordings, such as CDs with subliminal affirmations to support positive self-talk.

One day we went to a ropes course. At this course, they had us do activities where we had to learn to trust ourselves and others. It was scary but at the same time it was exhilarating. There was one point where felt like I couldn't do it and I tried and failed. But I asked to do it again. I succeeded the second time. The feeling that I got from that was so incredible. It was the first real self-esteem, not arrogance or ego, that I felt about myself in a really long time.

I also learned about setting goals for myself. My therapist encouraged me and empowered me with exercises and assignments. These exercises and the ropes course have since given me the courage to try things that I failed at before; for example, college. Later this year I am graduating at the top of my class.

Ali G., Recovering Addict

Trauma RELEASE TECHNIQUE (TRT)

TRT is a new treatment developed by one of the forefathers of holistic addiction treatment, John Giordano. TRT incorporates the healing effects of EMDR, the language realignment impact of NLP, and the soothing effects of hypnotherapy into a very effective therapy for victims of trauma. There is also evidence that TRT can help individuals suffering from blocks, such as performance slumps and test anxiety.

EMDR stands for eye movement desensitization and reprocessing. It is a method of dealing with trauma and unresolved issues. An unresolved issue is a past event that continues to cause us pain and suffering and continues to impact our future. It works by helping to process distressing memories more fully, which then reduces the distress caused by the memories. The eye movements used in EMDR have shown to decrease the vividness of the disturbing memory. Reducing the strength of the memory also reduces the emotions that go with the memory. In turn, any physical signs of stress associated with the memory, such as increased heart rate, high blood pressure, confusion, and other fear responses, are also reduced.

NLP stands for neurolinguistic programming. NLP deals with the networks of the brain associated with language and the impact of language on beliefs, feelings, and behaviors. Including hypnotherapy into the process of TRT allows suggestions for new feelings, attitudes, and behaviors to take hold.

Hypnosis is a trancelike state in which you have heightened focus, concentration, and inner absorption. When you're under hypnosis, you usually feel calm and relaxed, and you can concentrate intensely on a specific thought, memory, feeling, or sensation while blocking out distractions. Hypnosis is sometimes called hypnotherapy, and when you are hypnotized, you're more open than usual to suggestions. This can be used therapeutically to modify your perceptions, behavior, sensations, and emotions and to improve your health and well-being.

> *When I was 16 years old I was raped. I was a virgin. After that, I felt so low, so bad, so broken that my life completely changed. I used drugs for the next 27 years after that. Eventually I lived on the street and was a prostitute. I was raped two more times during the years I lived on the street. When I went to treatment, John did his TRT on me. Afterward, I no longer felt the emotional pain every time I thought about the rapes. The nightmares stopped. I was able to talk about them and process them during my therapy sessions. I have even included them in my step-work and begun to forgive the people who hurt me. I am so grateful that TRT allowed me to move beyond events in my life that made me feel so broken.*
>
> -recovering addict with 6 years clean

During the TRT therapy, you will be asked to remember and recount the trauma or disturbing memory. However, you will not be asked to relive the event. The purpose of the therapy is to put the event squarely in your past, where it belongs. When the traumatic event no longer seems like it is happening all over again each time you think of it, you can begin to process it effectively with your therapist. Ultimately TRT allows us to move beyond our past and to redesign our future, and this is what recovery is all about.

HEAVY METAL TOXICITY AND RECOVERY

Every toxic substance has the ability to damage our body, and usually the damage is worse the greater the extent of the exposure. Studies suggest that even small amounts of toxins can have profound effect on nervous system. The idea of toxic load grew out of physicians' observations that small exposures to more than one toxic substance often resulted in large damaging effects on the body. The body breaks down these toxins to get rid of them; however, excess or constant exposure occurs when the accumulation of toxins exceeds the ability to eliminate them and causes toxicity.

The presence of toxic metals in our systems is highly significant, for they are capable of causing serious health problems through interference with normal biological functioning. Although they can be found in high concentrations in the body, a number of these heavy metals (aluminum, beryllium, cadmium, lead, and mercury) have no known biological function. Others (arsenic, copper, iron, and nickel) are thought to be essential at low concentrations but are toxic at higher levels.

Heavy metals can disrupt metabolic function in two basic ways:

1. They accumulate and thereby disrupt function in vital organs and glands, such as heart, brain, kidneys, bones, liver, etc.

2. They replace vital nutritional minerals from where they should be in the body to provide biological function. For example, enzymes are catalysts for virtually every biochemical reaction in all life-sustaining processes of metabolism. But instead of calcium being present in an enzyme reaction chain, lead or cadmium may be there in its place. Toxic metals can't fulfill the same role as the nutritional minerals, thus their presence becomes critically disruptive to enzyme activity.

In our daily living, circumstances expose us to heavy metals. Limiting exposure as much as possible is important. Be aware that there are many ways toxins can be absorbed through skin, foods, beverages, and the air we breathe. Many use protective gloves and breathing aids; however, while these measures are helpful, they do not always give the protection needed.

Some of the sources and effects of Heavy Metals are listed below. The most toxic heavy metals are Aluminum, Arsenic, Antimony, Cadmium, Lead, Mercury:		
Heavy Metal	Sources	Effects
Aluminum	Found in beer, bleached flours, cookware, cigarette filters, auto exhaust, deodorants, dental amalgams, tobacco smoke	dementia at high levels, behavioral problems, colitis, dry skin, energy loss, headaches, heartburn, leg twitching, numbness
Arsenic	Found in burning materials, coal combustion, tobacco, pesticides, water, tobacco smoke	eating disorders, brittle nails, chronic anemia, burning in mouth, confusion, nervousness, swallowing difficulty, sweet metallic taste in mouth, hair loss
Antimony	found in tobacco, cocaine, textile manufacturing, hazardous waste sites, some toys made overseas	poor concentration, irritability, fatigue, respiratory disorders, GI Tract disorders

Cadmium	tobacco products, marijuana, airborn industrial contaminents, batteries, cigarette smoke, colas, dental alloys	poor concentration, migraines, cavities, high cholesterol, addiction to alcohol, hypoglycemia and attention concerns
Lead	cocaine, paint in old homes, colored inks, cosmetics, eating utensils, tobacco smoke, tobacco and filters	recent study shows high lead levels can lower IQ by as much as 10 points; learning disorders, Parkinson disease, calcium and iron deficiency, seizures
Mercury	tobacco, adhesives, battery manufacturing, broken thermometers, building materials, industrial waste, amalgams, polluted water, lens solutions, tattooing, wood preservatives, tuna and swordfish	allergies, eating disorders, depression, dizziness, emotional disturbances, adrenal dysfunction, scattered thinking, feeling overwhelmed

The presence of heavy metals can result from an accident, long-term exposure from environmental sources, or alcohol and drugs, including prescriptions and may cause depression, anxiety, suicidal ideations, which may lead to addictions. Ultimately, heavy metals can result in reduced quality of life.

The good news is that detoxification is possible. There are many products (with evidence-based research) that, in a supported program, provide an easy-to-follow detoxification plan. This program detoxifies heavy metal and toxins over a month, three months or a year, depending on the individual toxic load. These programs provide lab testing, educational materials, and full support for individuals on their path to health and wellness. Be sure to find a detoxification program that includes retesting and coaching to help maintain the best effects.

PREVENTING RELAPSE

STRATEGY FOR THE DAY

◊ Get up in the morning and say a prayer to your Higher Power. If not, pray for GOD (good orderly direction).

◊ Take five minutes to meditate in order to prepare for your day.

◊ Do your best to maintain positive self-talk. That means no negative thoughts, words, or actions. Okay, I know it's difficult! Just do your best. Seek progress, not perfection.

◊ Exercise: walking, swimming, weight lifting, etc.

◊ Stay away from caffeine and drink decaffeinated coffee if you must drink coffee.

◊ Go to meetings and sit in the front. Get to the meeting (AA/NA/GA/OA) five minutes early. At the meeting, if you are unsure of what you want to say, then just raise your hand and tell everyone that you're new and are just learning how to share.

◊ Stay five minutes after allowing people to get to know you and get phone numbers and dial them. Don't file them.

STEPS TO BUILDING A NEW LIFE

1. Maintain a recovery lifestyle. Follow the suggestions in this book as well as the self-help text (AA/NA/GA/OA).

2. Turn your focus inward. Become grounded in who you would like to become. Write down your values, likes, and dislikes. Write down your wants and needs. A want is something you would like. A need is a necessity. If you don't know what you want or need, then write down all the things you don't want or need, and see what's left. Then go from there.

3. Regarding relationships, you should write down, as best you can, your character defects. Be thorough. Ask people who really know you, preferably people who have your best interest at heart. Be prepared! You may not like what you hear. It's not about likes or dislikes. It's about gathering information. The more information, the better and more effective we will become with family, friends, and significant others. Keep in mind you are gathering information so you can better yourself. Reach out to your friends, relatives, and your significant other, provided you still have one. The more information you gather, the better you can understand the changes that may need to be made. Find

your weaknesses and your strengths and then reach out for help. Keep reaching out until you receive the answers you need in order for you to grow and change.

4. It has been my experience that addicts and alcoholics are usually very intelligent. It doesn't matter whether we learned it in the streets or in school. We learned how to live and survive in the world in spite of the odds. Now it is time to improve ourselves and enjoy a much better quality of life, free from whatever behavior or substance that we allowed to keep us prisoner. By exploring who we are and what we became, along with what we like and dislike, only then can we live the quality of life that God intended us to have.

5. Patience, consistency, commitment, and desire are just a few of the qualities we need to develop in order to be successful in anything. Keep reaching out and looking inward. More will be revealed.

6. Thoughts and ideas are great; reaching out to others is wonderful. Reading and educating yourself is noble, but without follow-up, all that good intent and initiative is for naught. Taking action is what brings cohesion to our lives. Because if you don't put all of this knowledge to use, what value does it hold? How can it possibly help you on your

journey? I believe you need to ask yourself, "What is preventing me from putting into action what I have learned?" Remember, it is a *we* program, not an *I* program. You never have to do anything alone again.

NEGATIVE SELF-TALK THAT PREVENTS US FROM BENEFITING FROM SELF-HELP GROUPS

One of the real barriers to recovery is our own mind! Negative self-talk prevents us from benefiting from self-help groups. Be alert to some of the following negative inner dialogues that often "tell us" to fail:

1. "These people are much sicker than I could ever be. I definitely don't belong here."
2. "This is a cult of fanatics. These people need to get a life!"
3. "Most of the people are probably drinking or getting high. I can't believe they are not doing anything."
4. "I can't see how listening to the stories can help me to stop using. It will probably just cause me to want to use more."
5. "I've never hit a bottom like some people. I can't relate. I've been successful, have money, and have never robbed anyone. *What am I doing here?*"
6. "I'm not stupid. I know what I have to do. I know I can quit using. I don't need someone else's help or support. I'm no weakling."
7. "I just did a little too much. I'll simply limit myself to smoking pot and drinking only

beer. I never got into too much trouble with only pot or beer."

8. "These people are religious freaks. I don't want to be part of this new religion. Where is God when you need him, anyway?"

9. "I don't do street drugs (yuck). My drugs are legal and acceptable to society. Besides, my (expensive) doctor prescribed them for me. So I went a little overboard a few times. Big deal!"

10. "These people's problems are nothing like mine. I only have two DUIs, not four like the guy next to me. My wife and I are only separated because she makes a big deal of my staying out getting high. At least I don't beat my wife like the guy in front of me. I would never get high with these kinds of people. The crack houses I go to have classier people than this."

A NEW LIFE WORTH LIVING

Confused on how to go about living a life of recovery? You are definitely not alone. Many before you had the same concerns. Will I be able to live without drugs and be happy? Can I maintain a recovery lifestyle? Where does my life go from here? So many questions, so few answers. Can I do it? So I want to do it? (Recovery). The questions will keep appearing. The good news is that most of your questions will be answered as time goes by.

Learning how to live takes time; being in a hurry will not make it happen any faster. Did you ever stop to think that you are already doing exactly what you need to do? Once you create movement, you then create change. The moment change occurs, opportunity occurs along with all kinds of possibilities. Staying free from drugs/ alcohol and risky behaviors creates an environment for healthy progress. Remember – progress, not perfection.

The program of recovery has an abundance of incredibly helpful information, which is based on favorable results: The knowledge of how to live and enjoy life on life's terms. Reach out to those who have come before you. Seek out the winners, the ones with long time abstinence, as well as a lifestyle of recovery. Recovery is not just about drugs and alcohol; it's about spirituality, balance, and finding your purpose in life, in order to become all that your creator intended you to be.

When you seek out the winners of recovery, remember that they are human beings who are struggling with their own character defects. Please don't place them on a pedestal, for you will only become disappointed. Your job is to keep what works for you and the discard the rest. Remember that you have choices. Take a risk and ask for help. It may be uncomfortable, but it won't kill you. The consequences of not asking for the help you need can and will be quite severe: death, institutions, and jails. And worst of all, living with your shame and guilt until you die. Following these simple suggestions will give you a life beyond your wildest dreams. You see, I know this to be true, I have that life!

TWELVE WAYS TO BE GOOD TO YOURSELF

1. Be part of the solution instead of the problem. Refuse to beat yourself up anymore. What good does it do anyway? Besides, it hurts.

2. Take it slow and easy; the new path you have chosen takes time to get used to. Learn to be patient or at least tolerant. Things change when you are consistent. The change is not about immediate gratification; it's about long-term meaningful gratification, not short-term fixes that don't really work.

3. Remember to give yourself positive strokes along the way. God knows how difficult it is to stay on a path of recovery, so be good to yourself. You've earned your accolades the same way you've earned your pain and suffering.

4. When you have loving thoughts toward yourself and others, you'll attract good energies back to yourself. I know you know what happens when our thoughts and actions are impure; we need only look around us at the messes our addictions brought upon us to be assured of this truth. Therefore, cultivate those good thoughts. Let them grow and help to heal you. Remember—progress, not perfection.

5. Refuse to criticize yourself or anyone else. Self-righteousness never was very becoming, and besides, all it gets you is rejection and low self-esteem. Addicts seem to enjoy being on a fault-finding mission with themselves and others.

6. Treat yourself to a hot bath, and light a scented candle. Put on your favorite relaxing music, and take a healthy break from the world. Oh! Don't worry, all your problems will still be there, and you can pick them back up if you choose to.

7. Go for a walk in the park or on the beach—anyplace where you can get back in touch with your gratitude for just being alive, clean, and sober. Reconnecting with the beauty of nature is a blessing in itself.

8. Seek out some warm and friendly conversations. If you can afford it, arrange a relaxing massage, along with some pleasant fragrances. Practice feeling good. God knows, we practice hard enough feeling bad.

9. Complete just one thing you said you were going to do. It doesn't matter how trivial. Just feel how it feels to keep your word again to yourself or to others.

10. Maintain an attitude of gratitude, for humility is definitely the way to spirituality and is a prerequisite for being open-minded and willing to change.

11. Learn to compliment yourself and others. It's a beautiful way of saying, "I notice your efforts." So often we notice our faults and everyone else's. It's time for changes. Appreciate life, and life will show its gratitude.

12. The ultimate way to feel good, I believe, is to reach out and help another human being. A phone call goes a long way. Just lend an ear to someone who is reaching out. It is the simple things that seem to have the most impact.

SUGGESTIONS

Get telephone numbers from other members and practice calling them. Get a sponsor who is at least three years clean and is active in the program. Meet with him or her at least once a week (male sponsor with male, female sponsor with female). After going to ninety meetings in ninety days, you can continue to go every day or cut back on your meetings. My suggestion is to go to four to five meetings per week. Work your steps. It is a therapeutic tool that will assist you on your journey.

Stay connected to the winners. Get involved. First build a strong foundation, and if you have to change anything after a year, then do it. It takes approximately eighteen months before your thoughts become clearly focused. Don't forget that when you stop using drugs, you then begin to heal. What you're dealing with is called post-acute withdrawal syndrome. So give time time. When you end your day, meditate and reflect on your day. Notice the difference between how you feel about yourself when you do uphold your program and values compared to how you feel when you compromise yourself.

Carry yourself with your shoulders back and head up high. It's difficult to feel depressed when your posture is held this way. I don't expect you to believe me, but just do it. If it doesn't work for you, don't do it.

Read these suggestions over and over again, and do your best to follow them. Don't worry if you don't do them perfectly, just do the work the best you can. The benefits will be hundredfold, I promise you! Do the best you can in following these suggestions; they're not meant to hurt you or control you. It's meant to help you to help yourself.

My hope for you is for you to become all that you can and to be the person God intended you to be. May your Higher Power continue to guide you on your journey, and remember, there are no coincidences. May these words of addicts and alcoholics who have come before you give you the strength and the courage to follow through and enjoy life one day at a time.

RELAPSE HISTORY

Please fill out your relapse history on the following two pages so you may see the sequence of events that lead toward making poor choices. When you are aware of your pathology, only then can you intervene and make changes that are necessary to stay on your path of recovery. So be thorough—your life depends upon it!

Look for your patterns; we all have them. Find the ones that are destructive, and also look for the ones that are beneficial. You might want to ask someone to help you to be objective. Please don't wait. Get busy!

Name:_____ Age:_____

Drugs of choice: _____

How long have you been clean from drugs and alcohol? _____

How much treatment have you had? _____

Number of different centers you attended. _____

Length of time in each? _____

How many times did you relapse? _____

What happened before you relapsed?

_____

What happened during your outing?

_____

What were your consequences after you relapsed?

_____

What caused you to get back on track?

_____

How did you feel when you made it back on the recovery path?

_____

RELAPSE PREVENTION QUESTIONNAIRE

This questionnaire will help you to assess your strengths and weaknesses. Please do your best to answer as objectively as possible. This will form the basis for your relapse prevention program and your treatment plan.

1. Do you attend a twelve-step fellowship (AA, NA, etc.)?
   Yes (2) __ No (0)__ Sometimes (1)__

2. How many meetings have you gone to in the last three months?
   60 or more (2)__ 30-59 (1)__ less than 30 (0)__

3. How many meetings have you gone to in the last two weeks?
   10 or more (2)__ 5-9 (1)__ less than 5 (0)__

4. Do you get angry about having to go to meetings?
   Yes (0)__ No (2)__ Sometimes (1)__
   If yes, give an explanation:

5. Are you involved in any twelve-step fellowship service (AA, NA, etc.)?
   Yes (2)__ No (0)__ Sometimes (1)__

6. Do you reach out at meetings to help any newcomers?
   Yes (2)__ No (0)__ Sometimes__

If yes or sometimes, when was the last time you did so?

7. Do you share at meetings?
    Yes (2)__ No (0)__ Sometimes (1)__
8. Out of the last ten meetings, how many times did you raise your hand and share? ___
9. Do you leave your twelve-step fellowship meetings before they are finished?
    Yes (0)__ No (2)__ Sometimes (1)__
    If yes or sometimes, Reasons

10. Do you go to meetings at least ten minutes early and stay until after they have finished?
    Yes (2)__ No (0)__ Sometimes (1)__
11. Do you go to meetings and find yourself always looking around and not paying attention?
    Yes (0)__ No (2)__ Sometimes (1)__
12. Are you bored at meetings?
    Yes (0)__ No (2)__ Sometimes (1)__
13. Do you go to any twelve-step fellowship social events?
    Yes (2) __ No (0)__ Sometimes (1)__
14. Have you done any twelve-step work in the last three months?

Yes (2) __ No (0)__ Sometimes (1)__

15. Do you have a home group?
Yes (2) __ No (0)__
If no, how come?

16. Do you go to meetings when you are not feeling emotionally well?
Yes (2) __ No (0)__ Sometimes (1)__
If no or sometimes, give brief explanation why you choose not to:

17. Do you slack off on attending your meetings because you're feeling good?
Yes (0) __ No (2)__ Sometimes (1)__
If yes or sometimes, give brief explanation why you choose not to:

18. Do you enjoy going to meetings?
Yes (2) __ No (0)__ Sometimes (1)__
If no or sometimes, give brief explanation of what you do not like:

19. Do you have a sponsor?
    Yes (2) __ No (0)__
    What action have you taken to get a sponsor?
    Give a brief explanation:

20. How long have you been clean or sober (free of all mood-altering substances)?

21. Do you feel comfortable with your current sponsor?
    Yes (2) __ No (0)__ Sometimes (1)__
    If no or sometimes, give a brief explanation for you discomfort:

22. How often do you call your sponsor?
    Daily (2)__ 3–6 days week (1)__ less than 3 times a week (0)__

23. Do you lie or tell half-truths to your sponsor?
    Yes (0)__ No (0)__ Sometimes (1)__
    If yes or sometimes, give brief explanation of what prevents you from being honest:

24. Does your sponsor encourage you to work the Twelve Steps of Recovery?
    Yes (2)___ No (0)__

25. Are you working the Twelve Steps of your recovery?
    Yes (2) __ No (1)__

26. What step are you on?

27. How long have you been working on this step?

28. Do you feel stuck on a particular step?
    Yes (0)__ No (0) Maybe (1)__

29. If yes or maybe, give a brief explanation:

30. What other steps are you having difficulty with, if any?

31. Is your sponsor helping you with your steps?

32. Yes (2)__ No (0)__ Sometimes (1)__

33. Does your sponsor encourage you to go to meetings?

34. Yes (2)__ No (0)__ Sometimes (1)__

35. How many meetings a week does your sponsor encourage you to attend?

36. Are you reaching out to others for help in working the steps?
Yes (2)__ No (0)__Sometimes (1)__

37. Do you feel you can get over on your sponsor?
Yes (0)__ No (2)__ Sometimes (1)__
If yes or sometimes, give a brief explanation how that makes you feel about yourself and your sponsor

38. Did you pick a sponsor that you felt would make you work on your recovery?
Yes (2)__ No (0)__

39. Did you pick a sponsor that you felt would not be so hard on you and that you could manipulate?
Yes (0)__ No (2)__

40. If you are not satisfied with your current sponsor, what steps have you taken to rectify this? Give a brief explanation:

41. How long have you known that you are dissatisfied with your sponsor?

42. How long has your sponsor been clean?

43. Do you sponsor anyone?
    Yes (2) __ No (0)__
    If yes, how many people?

44. Are you feeling overwhelmed or uncomfortable sponsoring these people?
    Yes (0)__ No (2)__ Sometimes (1)__
    If yes or sometimes, give a brief explanation for your discomfort:

45. Are you sponsoring anyone of the opposite sex?
    Yes (0)__ No (2)__ Sometimes (1)__
    If yes or sometimes, give a brief description of the circumstances and your reasoning:

46. Do you, as a sponsor, feel you are setting a good example of recovery?
    Yes (2)__ No (0)__ Sometimes (1)__
    If no or maybe, give a brief explanation for the way you feel:

47. What do you need to change to become a better sponsor?

48. Give a brief explanation of what being a sponsor means to you and what you expect from a sponsor.

49. Do you drink coffee or tea?
    Yes (0)__ No (2)__ Sometimes (1)__
    If yes, give amounts you drink on a daily basis:

50. Do you drink espresso or Cuban coffee?
    Yes (0)__ No (2)__ Sometimes (1)__
    If yes, give amounts you drink on a daily basis:

51. Do you drink soda with caffeine?
    Yes (0)__ No (2)__ Sometimes (1)__
    If yes, give amounts you drink on a daily basis:

52. Do you eat chocolate or any products made with chocolate?
    Yes (0)__ No (2)__ Sometimes (1)__

    If yes, how much and how often? Explain:

53. Do you use white sugar (refined sugar) or products that have white sugar in them?
    Yes (0)__ No (2)__ Sometimes (1)__
    If yes, what kind, how often and how much on an average day?

54. Do you eat white flour products? (bagels, white bread, cake, etc.)
    Yes (0)__ No (2)__ Sometimes (1)__
    If yes, what kind, how often and how much on an average day?

55. Do you find yourself craving sweets when you feel stressed or happy?
Yes (0)__ No (2)__ Sometimes (1)__

56. Do you smoke or use any other form of Tobacco?
Yes (0)__ No (2)__ Sometimes (1)__
If yes, how much, how often and what kind of Tobacco? Also, include how long you have been using tobacco:

57. Do you eat past 7:00 p.m.?
Yes (0)__ No (2)__ Sometimes (1)__
If yes or sometimes, how often in a week? Is it a heavy, medium, or light meal? Please describe each meal.

58. How long before you go to sleep do you eat? Explain:

59. Do you eat red meat?
Yes__No__

More than once a week?
Yes__No__

60. Do you eat three good meals a day?
    Yes (0)__ No (2)__ Sometimes (1)__
    If no, how many meals do you eat in an average day and describe briefly what these meals consist of:

61. Do you take any vitamins or supplements?
    Yes (2)__ No (0)__ Sometimes (1)__
    If yes, what kind, how often and when are they taken? When was the last time taken?

62. Have you ever been checked for hyper or hypoglycemia?
    Yes__ No__
63. Last check up? If you have it, what are you doing for it?

64. Do you have any medical illnesses that you know of?
    If yes, explain

65. Do you exercise regularly?
    Yes (2)__ No (0)__ Sometimes (1)__
    If yes or sometimes, describe what kind
    of exercise and how often you work out in
    a week.

66. Also, what average length of time you spend
    exercising, and when was the last time you
    worked out? If no, give reasons why you do
    not work out:
    a. Do you sweat when you work out?
        Yes (2)__ No (0)__ Sometimes (1)__
    b. What do you like or dislike about exercise?

    c. Do you consider yourself overweight?
        Yes (2)__ No (0)__ Maybe a little (1)__
        If yes, how many pounds do you feel you
        need to lose for you to feel comfortable?

    d. If under weight, how many pounds do
        you feel you have to gain?

67. Do you consider yourself a compulsive eater?
    Yes (0)__ No (2)__ Sometimes (1)__
68. Do you eat in excess when you feel stressed?
    Yes (0)__ No (2)__ Sometimes (1)__
    If yes or sometimes, give a brief explanation:

69. Do you overeat when you are feeling good?
    Yes (0)__ No (2)__ Sometimes (1)__
    If yes or sometimes, give a brief explanation:

70. Do you overeat to get back at someone?
    Yes (0)__ No (2)__ Sometimes (1)__
    If yes or sometimes, give a brief explanation:

71. Do you have a job or own your own business?
    Yes (2) __ No (0)__
72. In an average week, how many hours per day
    do you work?

73. Do you bring work home?
    Yes (0)__ No (2)__

If yes, how often:

74. Is your mind preoccupied with your job?
    Always (0)__ Sometimes (1)__ Rarely (0)__
75. Do you find yourself obsessing about making money?
    Always (0)__ Sometimes (1)__ Rarely (0)__
76. Are you happy with the work you are doing?
    Yes (2)__ No (0)__ Sometimes (1)__
    If no or sometimes, give a brief explanation:

77. List alternatives you have in order to increase your work satisfaction:

78. Have you taken any action?
    Yes__ No__
    If yes, give a brief explanation of what action you took:

79. What kind of work would you like to do (work in sales, with your hands, etc.)?

80. What is preventing you from doing this?

81. Are you married?
Yes__ No__
If yes, how long?

82. Are you in a relationship?
Yes__ No__

83. Briefly describe what you consider to be a healthy relationship:

84. Is your relationship monogamous?
Yes__ No__ Sometimes__
If no or sometimes, explain last outside encounter and how you felt afterward:

85. How many times in an average day do you find yourself looking at or daydreaming about people in a sexual way?

86. How much of your time do you feel is spent on these thoughts? Give approximate time?

87. Do you find the frequency increasing during times of stress?
Yes (0) __ No (2)__ Sometimes (1)__
During times of boredom?
Yes (0) __ No (2)__ Sometimes (1)__
When you are feeling good about yourself?
Yes (0) __ No (2)__ Sometimes (1)__
Give a brief explanation:

88. Do you feel you need a relationship in order to be complete?
Yes (0)__ No (2)__ Sometimes (1)__
If yes or sometimes, give a brief explanation:

89. Do you masturbate?
Yes __ No __ Sometimes __
If yes, how often in an average week?

90. Do you find yourself masturbating more often during times of stress?
Yes (0)__ No (2)__ Sometimes (1)
During times of boredom?
Yes (0)__ No (2)__ Sometimes (1)__
When you are feeling good about yourself?
Yes (0)__ No (2)__ Sometimes (1)__
Give a brief explanation:

91. Do you use sex to cover up or change your feelings?
Yes (0)__ No (2)__ Sometimes (1)__
Give a brief explanation:

92. List what you enjoy doing for fun (fishing, tennis, etc.)?

93. When was the last time you did something for fun?

94. In the last thirty days, how often did you do something for fun?

95. What did you do for fun?

96. Were other people involved in this activity?

97. How often in the last thirty days did you have fun with other people?

98. How often in the last thirty days did you have fun doing things alone?

99. Do you prefer doing these activities alone or with others?
    Give a brief explanation:

100. Do you believe in a Higher Power?
     Yes (2)___ No (0)___
101. How often do you pray to your Higher Power?
     Every day (2)___ Sometimes (1)___ Rarely or Never (0)___

If sometimes or rarely, give a brief explanation for your infrequency:

102. Do you pray for your will?
Yes (2)__ No (0)__ Sometimes (1)__
Give a brief explanation for your answer:

103. Do you feel a Higher Power can help you?
Yes (2)__ No (0)__ Sometimes (1)__
If yes, how do you expect your Higher Power to help you?

104. Do you pray to your Higher Power mostly when you are in trouble?
Yes (2)__ No (0)__ Sometimes (1)__

105. Do you pray to your Higher Power when things are going well?
Yes (2)__ No (0)__ Sometimes (1)__
If yes or sometimes, give reason why:

106. Do you feel you need to get more in touch with a Higher Power?
Yes (0)__ No (2)__ Sometimes (1)__

107. Are you working on improving you relationship with your Higher Power?
Yes (2)__ No (0)__ A little (1)__
Give a brief explanation for your answer:

108. Do you feel you practice humility when you pray?
Yes (2)__ No (0)__ Sometimes (1)__
If no or sometimes, give brief explanation why you do not:

109. Do you concentrate and are you sincere when you pray?
Yes (2)__ No (0)__ Sometimes (1)__
If no or sometimes, describe reason and circumstances for your attitude:

110. Do you meditate or allow yourself some quiet time away from everyone and everything?
Yes (2)__ No (0)__ Sometimes (1)__
If yes or sometimes, how often? If no, give a brief explanation for not practicing:

111. How do you meditate or practice quiet time?
Give a brief explanation:

112. Are you a grateful recovering person?
Yes (2)__ No (0)__ Sometimes (1)__
Is yes or sometimes, explain why:

113. Do you have trouble making friends?
Yes (2)__ No (0)__ Sometimes (1)__
If yes or sometimes, explain why you think it is hard for you: What action have you been taking to change this?

114. Do you find yourself feeling lonely (choose from last experience)?
Often (0)__ Sometimes (1)__ Hardly Ever (2)__
If you answered often or sometimes, describe what action you took to address this feeling and how it helped? If you took little or no action, explain, as best you can why

115. Do you find yourself bored (choose from last experience)?
Often (0)__ Sometimes (1)__ Hardly Ever (2)__
If often or sometimes, describe what action was taken to address this feeling and how it helped. If little or no action was taken explain, as best you can, why?

116. Do you find yourself feeling overwhelmed (choose from last experience)?
Often (0)__ Sometimes (1)__ Hardly Ever (2) __
If you answered often or sometimes, describe what action you took to address this feeling and how it helped. If no or very little action was taken, explain, as best you can, why?

117. Do you gamble?
Yes (0)__ No (2)__ Sometimes (1)__
If yes or sometimes, how often in an average thirty day period?

118. How much did you spend?

119. Could you afford to spend that much?

120. Do you find yourself gambling more when you are?
Angry __ Bored __ Lonely__ Depressed__
Happy__Doesn't matter__

121. Do you feel you are a compulsive gambler?
Yes (0)__ No (2)__ Sometimes (1)__
Explain your answer briefly

122. Do you find yourself shopping for things you do not need?
Yes (0)__ No (2)__ Sometimes (1)__
If yes or sometimes, briefly explain why

123. Do you find yourself shopping more when you are?
Angry__ Bored__ Lonely__ Depressed__
Happy__Does not matter__

124. Do you buy things you don't need and then regret it?

     Yes (0)__ No(2)__ Sometimes (1)__

     If yes or sometimes, briefly explain your answer:

125. Do you consider yourself a compulsive shopper?

     Yes (0)__ No (2)__ Sometimes (1)__

     If yes or sometimes, briefly explain your answer:

Score_____ (Total all answers)

80 or higher	You are doing well—keep it up!
65- 79	Needs improvement, but don't give up. Keep working on yourself. It will get better.
50–64	Headed for trouble. Reach out, get some help. *You are never alone.*
Less than 50	You are in relapse mode. Chances are good that if you don't do something, you will relapse—or maybe you already have. Call a local helpline, or reach out to us at John Giordano 786-271-5732 holisticaddictioninfo.com.

IDENTIFIED PROBLEMS

Summary/ Evaluation of Your Recovery

_____

_____

_____

_____

_____

_____

_____

_____

_____

_____

_____

_____

_____

_____

_____

_____

_____

_____

IMMEDIATE GOALS

Time frame when they will start
and when they will be completed.

1. _____
_____
_____

2. _____
_____
_____

3. _____
_____
_____

4. _____
_____
_____

5. _____
_____
_____

6. _____
_____
_____

LONG-TERM GOALS

Give estimated beginning and completion dates

_____

_____

_____

_____

_____

_____

_____

_____

_____

_____

GO FOR IT!!!

Telephone Numbers

AL-ANON Family Headquarters: 757-563-1600
G & G Holistic Addiction Treatment
A Holistic Approach to Addiction: John Giordano
786-271-5732 holisticaddictioninfo.com
Rational Recovery: 916-621-2667
National number for AA: 212-647-1680
National number for NA: 818-773-9999

Addictions
Alcoholics Anonymous: 212-810-3400
Narcotics Anonymous: 818-773-9999
Co-dependents Anonymous: 602-277-7991
Debtors Anonymous: 212-642-8220
Gamblers Anonymous Hotline: 800-397-9843
National Cocaine Hotline: 800-262-2463
Overeaters Anonymous: 505-891-2664
AIDS Hotline: 1-800-342-2437
Spanish AIDS Hotline: 1-800-344-7432

HOLISTIC ADDICTION TREATMENT VITAMINS

The following section details information about our proprietary nutritional and amino acid formulations called nutraceuticals. We have spent many years researching and perfecting these formulations. Mental Clarity and SynaptaGenX have been studied with the same scrutiny and many of the same methods required for FDA approval. In summary, we have found both products to be effective support tools for recovery.

To learn more about our nutritional supplements, visit John Giordano 786-271-5732 holisticaddictioninfo.com

For more information and research articles, visit http://www.holisticaddictioninfo.com or see the suggested readings section of this book.

ANTI ANXIETY SLEEP FORMULA

This blend of ingredients is designed to help enhance peace and serenity when taken in low dosages. The ingredients are designed to mitigate or diminish the body's stress response and therefore lessen the detrimental effects of stress. At a higher dosage, it may be taken in the evening to support restful sleep. The antianxiety/ sleep formula calms the nervous system and helps to establish a healthy sleep pattern. Sleep deprivation interrupts the natural restoration cycle and robs the body of nutrients, causing serious deterioration in performance of body functions. Healthy rest and sleep cycles improve the body's immune response and ability to heal. The supplements in our formula aid the body in achieving a deeper and more restful sleep.

1. Vitamin B6 (pyridoxine HCl) is involved in the formation of body proteins and structural compounds, including chemical

transmitters in the brain. Vitamin B6 is also critical in maintaining hormonal balance and proper immune function. Deficiency of Vitamin B6 is characterized by depression, glucose intolerance, anemia, impaired nerve function, cracking of the lips and tongue, and seborrhea or eczema.

2. Valerian Root—Valerian (<u>nervous</u>)—has been used as a sleep aid for over 1,000 years. Its ability to help relax the central nervous system, promote feelings of calm, decrease levels of anxiety and stress, and enhance sleep are known to millions the world over. Unlike some prescription sleep aids, valerian is not known to cause morning grogginess and is non-addictive. Time-release technology offers a steady release of valerian for 6–8 hours, ensuring better, more restful sleep.

3. Skullcap herb is one of the most widely relevant nervines available. It relaxes states of nervous tension while at the same time renewing and revitalizing the central nervous system. It has a specific use in the treatment of seizure and hysterical states as well as epilepsy.

4. L-Theanine is a non-protein amino acid mainly found naturally in the green tea plant (Camellia sinensis). L-theanine is the predominant amino acid in green tea and

makes up 50% of the total free amino acids in the plant. The amino acid constitutes between 1% and 2% of the dry weight of green tea leaves. L-theanine is considered the main component responsible for the taste of green tea, which in Japanese is called umami. L-theanine is marketed in Japan as a nutritional supplement for mood modulation.

5. Passion Flower bears small berry-like fruit called granadilla or water lemon. The plant is native to North, Central, and South America. While primarily tropical, some of its 400 species can grow in colder climates. The plant is also nicknamed Maypop, descriptive of the popping sound the fruit makes when mashed. Passion Flower was first investigated scientifically less than 100 years ago when it was found to possess an analgesic (pain-killing) property, and to prevent, without side effects, sleeplessness caused by brain inflammation. Since then, the sedative properties of Passion Flower have been observed and documented in many studies. Primary chemical constituents of this herb include alkaloids (harman, harmine, harmaline, harmol, harmalol), flavonoids (apigenin, luteolin, quercitin, rutin), flavone glycosides, sterols, sugars, and gums. The flavonoids in Passion Flower

are primarily responsible for its relaxing and anti-anxiety effects.

6. Chamomile is one of the safest medicinal herbs, chamomile is a soothing, gentle relaxant that has been shown to work for a variety of complaints from stress to menstrual cramps. This herb has a satisfying, apple-like aroma and flavor (the name chamomile is derived from the Greek kamai melon, meaning ground apple), and it's most often taken as a delicious, mild therapeutic tea.

7. Melatonin is a hormone (N-acetyl-5 methoxytryptamine) produced especially at night in the pineal gland, a structure in the brain. Its secretion is stimulated by the dark and inhibited by light. Tryptophan is converted to serotonin and finally converted to melatonin, which is an Indole.

8. Lemon Balm has mild sedative properties and has been used to relieve gas, reduce fever, and increase perspiration. The volatile oil contains citral, citronellal, eugenol acetate and geraniol. Both oil and hot water extracts of the leaves have been shown to possess strong antibacterial and antiviral qualities.

To learn more about our nutritional supplements, visit John Giordano 786-271-5732 holisticaddictioninfo.com.

For more information and research articles visit http://www.holisticaddictioninfo.com or see the suggested readings section of this book.

MULTIVITAMINS MINERAL
SELF-DEFENSE

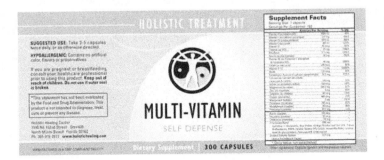

This formulation supplies essential vitamins and minerals that are needed to support tissue repair and restoration and is fortified with probiotics and digestive enzymes to support healthy digestion, absorption, and elimination. The multivitamin mineral formula helps to balance the nervous system and strengthen the whole body. The proper combination of minerals, antioxidants, and vitamins is essential for healthy, normal metabolism, growth, and longevity. The whole food vitamins in our formula supply individual cells with the nutrients they need to flourish.

1. Copper (sulfate): The human body contains only 70 to 80 mg of copper in total, but it's an essential part of many important enzymes. Copper's possible role in treating disease is

based on the fact that these enzymes can't do their jobs without it.

2. Manganese (sulfate): Our bodies contain only a very small amount of manganese, but this metal is important as a constituent of many key enzymes. The chemical structure of these enzymes is interesting: large protein molecules cluster around a tiny atom of metal. Manganese plays a particularly important role as part of the natural antioxidant enzyme super oxide dismutase (SOD), which helps fight damaging free radicals. It also helps energy metabolism, thyroid function, blood sugar control, and normal skeletal growth.

3. Chromium (picolinate): Chromium is a mineral the body needs in very small amounts, but it plays a significant role in human nutrition. Chromium's most important function in the body is to help regulate the amount of glucose (sugar) in the blood. Insulin plays a starring role in this fundamental biological process by regulating the movement of glucose out of the blood and into cells. Scientists believe that insulin uses chromium as an assistant (technically, a cofactor) to "unlock the door" to the cell membrane, thus allowing glucose to enter the cell.

4. Molybdenum (Na molybdenate): Small amounts of this element are essential.

5. Potassium (chloride): Potassium is one of the major electrolytes in your body, along with sodium and chloride. Potassium and sodium work together like a molecular seesaw: when the level of one goes up, the other goes down. All together, these three dissolved minerals play an intimate chemical role in every function of your body.

6. Vanadium (chelate): Vanadium, a mineral, is named after the Scandinavian goddess of beauty, youth, and luster. Taking vanadium will not make you beautiful, youthful, and lustrous, but evidence from animal studies suggests it may be an essential micronutrient. That is, your body may need it, but in very low doses.

7. Boron (chelate): Boron aids in the proper metabolism of vitamins and minerals involved with bone development, such as calcium, copper, magnesium, and vitamin D. In addition, boron appears to affect estrogen and possibly testosterone as well, hormones that affect bone health. On this basis, boron has been suggested for preventing or treating osteoporosis. However, there have been no clinical studies to evaluate the potential benefits of boron supplements for any bone-related conditions. On the

basis of similarly weak evidence, boron is often added to supplements intended for the treatment of osteoarthritis. Boron has also been proposed as a sports supplement, based on its effects on hormones. However, studies have, as yet, failed to find evidence that it helps increase muscle mass or enhances performance.

8. Choline (bitartrate): Choline has only recently been recognized as an essential nutrient. Choline is part of the neurotransmitter acetylcholine, which plays a major role in the brain; for this reason, many studies have been designed to look at choline's role in brain function.

Choline functions as a part of a major biochemical process in the body called methylation; choline acts as a methyl donor.

Until recently, it was thought that the body could use other substances to substitute for choline, such as folate, vitamins B_6 and B_{12}, and the amino acid methionine. But recent evidence has finally shown that, for some people, adequate choline supplies cannot be maintained by other nutrients and must be obtained independently through diet or supplements.

9. Vitamin A: Vitamin A plays an important role in vision, bone growth, reproduction, cell division and cell differentiation. It helps

maintain the surface linings of the eyes and the respiratory, urinary, and intestinal tracts. When those linings break down, bacteria can enter the body and cause infection. Vitamin A also helps maintain the integrity of skin and mucous membranes that function as a barrier to bacteria and viruses. Vitamin A helps regulate the immune system. The immune system helps prevent or fight off infections by making white blood cells that destroy harmful bacteria and viruses. Vitamin A may help lymphocytes, a type of white blood cell that fights infections, function more effectively.

10. Vitamin C (Ester C): Ester-C™ is a patented form of Vitamin C that is pH-balanced and time-released. It is a patented form of ascorbyl palmitate. An ester, in general, is the combination of an acid and an alcohol. With Ester-C™, the acid is ascorbic acid (vitamin C). Ester-C™ is the premium brand of vitamin C esters available. It differs from other Vitamin C in that it will not give you an acid stomach and it will give you the benefits of Vitamin C over a longer period of time. It is also more bioavailable than other Vitamin C. Vitamin C is required for the synthesis of collagen, an important structural component of blood vessels, tendons, ligaments, and bone.

Vitamin C also plays an important role in the synthesis of the neurotransmitter, norepinephrine. Neurotransmitters are critical to brain function and are known to affect mood. In addition, vitamin C is required for the synthesis of carnitine, a small molecule that is essential for the transport of fat to cellular organelles called mitochondria, for conversion to energy Recent research also suggests that vitamin C is involved in the metabolism of cholesterol to bile acids, which may have implications for blood cholesterol levels and the incidence of gallstones.

11. Vitamin E (Tocopherols): Vitamin E is any of several fat soluble vitamins that are chemically tocopherols. Vitamin E is a popular and powerful antioxidant. Vitamin E is effective in preventing the oxidation of polyunsaturated fatty acids. Additionally, Vitamin E is helpful in the prevention of oxidation in the lungs, where strong oxidizing agents nitrogen dioxide and ozone, components of air pollution, are particularly harmful to people exercising. Vitamin E protects white and red blood cells, helping the body's immune system.

12. Thiamin (Vitamin B1): The need for Thiamin (Vitamin B1) in the body is mainly for the breakdown and utilization of carbohydrates

and fats. As discussed earlier, carbohydrates (as glucose) are the body's main source of energy. Every cell in our body is dependent on glucose produced for energy. However, the body's ability to convert carbohydrates into glucose is interdependent with enzymes and coenzymes. For example, acting as coenzyme, Thiamin works in converting carbohydrates into glucose for energy, and every single cell of your body requires that energy.

13. Riboflavin (Vitamin B2): It is required by the body to use oxygen and the metabolism of amino acids, fatty acids, and carbohydrates. Riboflavin is further needed to activate vitamin B6 (pyridoxine), helps to create niacin, and assists the adrenal gland. It may be used for red blood cell formation, antibody production, cell respiration, and growth.

14. Niacinamide: Vitamin B3 is required for cell respiration, helps in the release of energy and metabolism of carbohydrates, fats, and proteins, proper circulation and healthy skin, functioning of the nervous system, and normal secretion of bile and stomach fluids. It is used in the synthesis of sex hormones, treating schizophrenia and other mental illnesses, and is a memory-enhancer.

15. Pyridoxine HCI (Vitamin B6): Vitamin B6 is involved in the formation of body proteins and structural compounds, including chemical transmitters in the brain. Vitamin B6 is also critical in maintaining hormonal balance and proper immune function. Deficiency of Vitamin B6 is characterized by depression, glucose intolerance, anemia, impaired nerve function, cracking of the lips and tongue, and seborrhea or eczema.

16. Folate (folic acid): Folic acid works along with vitamin B12 and vitamin C to help the body digest and utilize proteins and to synthesize new proteins when they are needed. It is necessary for the production of red blood cells and for the synthesis of DNA (which controls heredity and is used to guide the cell in its daily activities). Folic acid also helps with tissue growth and cell function. In addition, it helps to increase appetite when needed and stimulates the formation of digestive acids.

17. Vitamin B12: It helps maintain healthy nerve cells and red blood cells, and is also needed to make DNA, the genetic material in all cells (1–4). Vitamin B12 is bound to the protein in food. Hydrochloric acid in the stomach releases B12 from protein during digestion. Once released, B12 combines

with a substance called intrinsic factor (IF) before it is absorbed into the bloodstream.

18. Biotin: Biotin is a water-soluble member of the B-complex group of vitamins and is commonly referred to as vitamin H. The biochemical acts as a carrier for carbon dioxide in the pyruvate carboxylase reaction, where biotin is linked to the epsilon-amino group of a lysine residue in the enzyme. Biotin is necessary for both metabolism and growth in humans, particularly with reference to production of fatty acids, antibodies, digestive enzymes, and in niacin (vitamin B-3) metabolism. Food sources for biotin are liver, kidney, soy flour, egg yolk, cereal, and yeast. There are suggestions that biotin is also capable of curing baldness, alleviating muscle pain and depression, and functions as a cure for dermatitis, although there is no substantial evidence for any of these claims. Biotin deficiency results in fatigue, depression, nausea, muscle pains, hair loss, and anemia

19. Pantothenic acid: Pantothenic acid (PA), a B-complex vitamin, is essential for humans and animals for growth, reproduction, and normal physiological functions. It is a precursor of the coenzymes, CoA and acyl carrier protein of fatty acid synthase, which are involved in more than 100

different metabolic pathways including energy metabolism of carbohydrates, proteins and lipids, and the synthesis of lipids, neurotransmitters, steroid hormones, porphyrins, and hemoglobin.

20. Calcium (carbonate and citrate): Calcium is essential to many body functions, including the transmission of nerve impulses, the regulation of muscle contraction and relaxation (including of the heart), blood clotting, and various metabolic activities. Calcium is also necessary for maintaining strong bones and is commonly prescribed to prevent and treat postmenopausal osteoporosis (bone thinning). Vitamin D, which aids in the absorption of calcium from the intestine, is often prescribed along with calcium supplements to prevent or treat osteoporosis. (Indeed, some calcium supplement tablets contain vitamin D.)

21. Iodine (potassium iodide): Iodine may be used when it is desirable to maintain a high level of beneficial iodides in the thyroid gland. Iodide is a form of iodine that is permanently taken up by the thyroid gland. This product also supports the body's normal detoxification processes, including the removal of heavy metals.

22. Magnesium (oxide): Magnesium is an essential nutrient, meaning that your body

needs it for healthy functioning. It is found in significant quantities throughout the body and used for numerous purposes, including muscle relaxation, blood clotting, and the manufacture of ATP (adenosine triphosphate, the body's main energy molecule).

23. Zinc (aspartate): Zinc is an important element that is found in every cell in the body. More than 300 enzymes in the body need zinc in order to function properly. Although the amount of zinc we need in our daily diet is tiny, it's very important that we get it. However, the evidence suggests that many of us do not get enough.

24. Selenium (sodium selenite): Selenium is a trace mineral that our bodies use to produce glutathione peroxidase. Glutathione peroxidase is part of the body's antioxidant defense system; it works with vitamin E to protect cell membranes from damage caused by dangerous, naturally occurring substances known as free radicals.

** Spirulina, choline bitartrate, bee pollen, citrus bioflavonoids, ginkgo biloba leaf extract 24 percent, panax ginseng root, PABA, gotu kola herb, CoQ10, betaine HCI, inositol, papain (1:2,000), bromelain 600 GDU, hesperidin, lipase 1,500 LU, rutin, licorice root, and octacosanol.

To learn more about our nutritional supplements, visit John Giordano 786-271-5732 holisticaddictioninfo.com.

For more information and research articles visit http://www.holisticaddictioninfo.com or see the suggested readings section of this book.

MENTAL CLARITY SELF-DEFENSE

The amino acid combination of this proprietary formulation is essential for restoring and rebuilding proper brain functioning. Continued use restores the energy, promotes clarity of thought, and improves focus and mental acuity. Energy drives all biological, physiological and chemical reactions in the body. Our intricate balance of food supplements with the proper quantity of vitamins, amino acids, and herbs results in efficient energy production. Memory deterioration is a result of insufficient supply of nutrients combined with increased free radical activity and poor circulation. Nutrients such as vitamin B, amino acids, and ginkgo biloba help to enhance memory by improving circulation and brain function.

1. DL-Phenylaline (DLPA): a 50/50 (equimolar) mixture of D-Phenylalanine and L-Phenylalanine. L-phenylalanine is an essential amino acid that can be converted

to L-Tyrosine by a complex biochemical process that takes place in the liver. L-Tyrosine can be converted by neurons in the brain to dopamine and norepinephrine (noradrenaline), hormones which are depleted by stress, overwork, and certain drugs. By replenishing norepinephrine in the brain, mental energy levels are enhanced, some forms of depression are alleviated, and a feeling of contentment often occurs. Because of the liver conversion necessary for L-phenylalanine to have these effects, L-Tyrosine is often faster acting. In addition, the conversion step from L-Tyrosine to norepinephrine may be enhanced if the cofactors (vitamins B6 and C) are included.

2. L-Tyrosine: a nonessential *amino acid* (protein building block) that the body synthesizes from *phenylalanine*, another amino acid. Tyrosine is important to the structure of almost all proteins in the body. It is also the precursor of several neurotransmitters, including L-dopa, dopamine, norepinephrine, and epinephrine. L-tyrosine, through its effect on neurotransmitters, may affect several health conditions, including *Parkinson's disease*, *depression*, and other mood disorders. Studies have suggested that tyrosine may help people with depression.

Preliminary findings indicate a beneficial effect of tyrosine, along with other amino acids, in people affected by dementia, including *Alzheimer's disease* Due to its role as a precursor to norepinephrine and epinephrine (two of the body's main stress-related hormones) tyrosine may also ease the adverse effects of environmental, psychosocial, and physical stress. L-tyrosine is converted by skin cells into melanin, the dark pigment that protects against the harmful effects of ultraviolet light. Thyroid hormones, which have a role in almost every process in the body, also contain tyrosine as part of their structure.

3. L-Glutamine: The extremely popular amino acid L-Glutamine can be found in protein powders, beans, meats, fish, poultry, dairy products, and of course, L-Glutamine supplements. Glutamine is highly in demand throughout the body. For years, athletes and bodybuilders have been looking for a product to help them recover faster from workouts and competition, keep their muscles well hydrated for maximum growth, and provide numerous other benefits in the muscle building process. In recent years, most athletes have come to understand the benefits of L-Glutamine.

L-Glutamine is the most abundant amino acid in the body and makes up more than 60% of the intramuscular amino acid pool. L-Glutamine plays an important role in many body functions such as proper immune system function, the transfer of nitrogen between organs, precursor to DNA, and regulation of protein synthesis and degradation. Following an intense workout, your body needs to replenish glutamine stores to aid in recovery. L-Glutamine can help increase muscle cell hydration and aid in protein synthesis. These and more functions of L-Glutamine can benefit athletes and bodybuilders by improving recovery and performance.

4. Taurine: an amino acid-like compound and a component of bile acids, which are used to help absorb fats and fat-soluble vitamins. Taurine also helps regulate the heartbeat, maintain cell membrane stability, and prevent brain cell over-activity.

5. Ginseng root, Korean / panax: True ginseng is in the genus Panax, which comes from the Latin word *panacea*. The type of ginseng typically used is of the species ginseng. Ginseng is used to treat a host of conditions, and, when it is taken daily, to maintain general good health. Ginseng has been shown in human studies to have a

long-term anti-stress effect and to improve physical and mental performance, memory, and reaction time.

6. L-Theanine: a non-protein amino acid mainly found naturally in the green tea plant (Camellia sinensis). L-theanine is the predominant amino acid in green tea and makes up 50% of the total free amino acids in the plant. The amino acid constitutes between 1% and 2% of the dry weight of green tea leaves. L-theanine is considered the main component responsible for the taste of green tea, which in Japanese is called umami. L-theanine is marketed in Japan as a nutritional supplement for mood modulation.

7. B6 Pyridoxine HCI: Vitamin B6 (Pyridoxine) is involved in the formation of body proteins and structural compounds, including chemical transmitters in the brain. Vitamin B6 is also critical in maintaining hormonal balance and proper immune function. Deficiency of Vitamin B6 is characterized by depression, glucose intolerance, anemia, impaired nerve function, cracking of the lips and tongue, and seborrhea or eczema.

8. Ginkgo Biloba Leaf Extract: supports the memory function; ginkgo also appears to support blood circulation to the brain,

thereby optimizing the amount of oxygen supplied to brain cells. It may also help increase blood flow to the extremities.

9. 5 HTP: The nutrient 5-HTP (the common name for the compound 5-hydroxytryptophan) is a derivative of the amino acid tryptophan. A mood-enhancing chemical, 5-HTP has attracted a good deal of attention lately because of its ability to increase pain tolerance, induce sleep, and affect how hunger is perceived. Unlike many other supplements (and drugs) that have molecules too large to pass from the bloodstream into the brain, molecules of 5-HTP are small enough to do so. Once in the brain, they're converted into an important nervous system chemical, or neurotransmitter, called serotonin.

The body produces its own supply of 5HTP from tryptophan, an amino acid found in high-protein foods such as chicken, fish, beef, and dairy products. Any healthy diet should include tryptophan-rich sources such as these.

To learn more about our nutritional supplements, visit John Giordano 786-271-5732 holisticaddictioninfo.com.

For more information and research articles visit http://www.holisticaddictioninfo.com or see the suggested readings section of this book.

SYNAPTAGENX

SynaptaGenX is a patented neuroadaptagen amino acid therapy that helps regulate cravings, promotes optimal brain health, neurotransmitter balance, focus and cognition, enhanced energy and reduced stress. SynaptaGenX is a result of over 30 years of research, including 23 clinical trials, led by Dr. Kenneth Blum, the pioneer of amino acid therapy for addiction recovery. SynaptaGenX utilizes a patented technology that maximizes body's ability to absorb the active ingredients quickly and easily. SynaptaGenX is an all-natural product which has been shown in numerous studies to promote dopamine, serotonin and endorphins—important chemicals in the brain responsible for feeling good. SynaptaGenX assists individuals with Reward Deficiency System (RDS) as described by Dr. Kenneth Blum, PhD. Individuals with RDS are unable to produce an adequate feeling of well-being and consequently often self-medicate with substances that help raise the levels of "feel-good" chemicals (i.e., dopamine) in their system—if only temporarily.

SynaptaGenX contains patented technology, which has been shown to reduce or eliminate excessive desires for unhealthy behaviors and pleasure-inducing substances, including psychostimulant use/abuse, alcohol, and excessive food cravings. The neuronutrients in SynaptaGenX help promote optimal dopamine function, normalize satiety and pleasure satisfaction from normally enjoyable activities and experiences, improve energy regulation, reduce stress, promote well-being, and increase feelings of happiness. For more information on reward deficiency syndrome, visit these sites:

http://www.rewarddeficiencysyndrome.com/
http://www.holisticaddictioninfo.com/
http://www.ncbi.nlm.nih.gov/pubmed?term=reward%20deficiency%20syndrome
http://www.iioab-journal.webs.com/

For more information on SynaptaGenX, visit these sites:
www.holisticaddictioninfo.com/
http://synaptagenx.com/

LIVER HEALTH SELF-DEFENSE

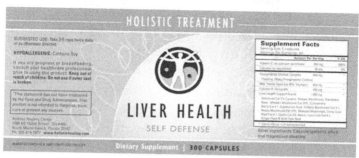

The liver is responsible for filtering and cleansing blood coming from the digestive tract before it reaches other parts of the body. The liver is a major organ for detoxifying the body and metabolizing drugs. The liver also makes proteins, which are important in many body functions.

This proprietary formulation has been used to help significantly lower hepatitis C viral load and detox and strengthen the liver. Herbal and nutritional supplements are combined to support liver health and gently but thoroughly detoxify the body naturally. This in turn reduces stress and strain on the liver.

1. Vitamin C (Ester C): Ester-C™ is a patented form of Vitamin C that is pH-balanced and time-released. It is a patented form of ascorbyl palmitate. An ester, in general, is the combination of an acid and an alcohol. With Ester-C™, the acid is ascorbic acid (vitamin C). Ester-C™

is the premium brand of vitamin C esters available. It differs from other Vitamin C's in that it will not give you an acid stomach and it will give you the benefits of Vitamin C over a longer period of time. It is also more bioavailable than other Vitamin C.

2. Phosophatidyl Choline Complex: Phytosomes are advanced forms of herbal products that are better absorbed, utilized, and, as a result, produce better results than conventional herbal extracts. Phytosomes are produced via a patented process whereby the individual components of an herbal extract are bound to phosphatidylcholine—an emulsifying compound derived from soy. Phosphatidylcholine is also one of the chief components of the membranes in our cells.

3. Milk Thistle Seed Ext.: Milk Thistle extract promotes healthy, vibrant liver function. The liver is one of the body's most important organs, since it helps rid the body of toxins that can impair good health. The active ingredient in milk thistle thought to give it its beneficial properties is called silymarin. The extract of milk thistle provides a guaranteed potency of 80% silymarin. It is an herb from a plant found in dry rocky soil in Europe and the U.S.

4. Calcium D-glucarate: Calcium D-glucarate is the *calcium* salt of D-glucaric acid, a

natural substance found in many *fruits* and *vegetables*.

Calcium D-glucarate has been shown to inhibit beta-glucuronidase, an enzyme found in certain bacteria that reside in the gut. One of the key ways in which the body eliminates toxic chemicals as well as hormones such as *estrogen* is by attaching glucuronic acid to them in the liver and then excreting this complex in the bile. Beta-glucuronidase is a bacterial enzyme that uncouples (breaks) the bond between the excreted compound and glucuronic acid. When beta-glucuronidase breaks the bond, the hormone or toxic chemical that is released is available to be reabsorbed into the body instead of being excreted. An elevated beta-glucuronidase activity is associated with an increased risk for various *cancers*, particularly hormone-dependent cancers like *breast*, *prostate*, and *colon*.

5. Artichoke ext 2% Cynarin: This large, thistle-like plant is native to the regions of southern Europe, North Africa, and the Canary Islands. The leaves of the plant are used medicinally. However, the roots and the immature flower heads may also contain beneficial compounds. Artichoke leaves contain a wide number of active constituents, including cynarin, 1,3 dicaffeoylquinic acid,

3-caffeoylquinic acid, and scolymoside. The choleretic (bile stimulating) action of the plant has been well documented in a controlled trial involving a small sample of healthy volunteers.

6. Maitake Mushroom ext 20%: Maitake has a high content of polysaccharide compound called Beta Glucan, which stimulates the activities of immune cells. It also contains valuable nutrients such as vitamin C, D, B2, niacin, minerals (especially magnesium, potassium and calcium), fiber and amino acids, and yet it is extremely low in calories, fat, and cholesterol. The whole mushroom shows benefits as a tonic and is specifically useful in:

◊ Lowering blood pressure
◊ Reducing serum cholesterol
◊ Lowering blood sugar
◊ Weight loss
◊ Constipation
◊ Uterine fibroids
◊ Stimulating cellular immunity
◊ Inhibiting tumor growth and metastasis
◊ Used during conventional cancer treatment to reduce side-effects such as hair loss, pain, fatigue and nausea

7. An isolated beta-glucan component, known as D-fraction, functions as a potent immune

modulator by boosting the body's own immune responses including natural killer cells, cytotoxic T-cells, macrophage, super oxide anion cells and interleukin.

**Schizandra berry Ext 4:1, shitake mushroom, dandelion root, bupleurum root, shitake mushroom ext 4:1, meitake mushroom, reishi mushroom ext 10:1, dong quai root ext 4:1, garlic clove ext 4:1, lycil fruit, ginger root, wild yam root

To learn more about our nutritional supplements, visit John Giordano 786-271-5732 holisticaddictioninfo.com

For more information and research articles visit http://www.holisticaddictioninfo.com or see the suggested readings section of this book.

LIVER HEALTH COMPANION

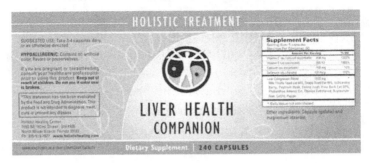

This powerful antioxidants formula complements the liver health formula for maximum efficacy. Ingredients support healthy digestion, reduce inflammation, boost immune system, and support overall wellness. It may also be used alone during times of stress for additional immune support.

1. Vitamin C (Ester C): Ester-C™ is a patented form of Vitamin C that is pH-balanced and time-released. It is a patented form of ascorbyl palmitate. An ester, in general, is the combination of an acid and an alcohol. With Ester-C™, the acid is ascorbic acid (vitamin C). Ester-C™ is the premium brand of vitamin C esters available. It differs from other Vitamin C's in that it will not give you an acid stomach and it will give you the benefits of Vitamin C over a longer period of time. It is also more bioavailable than other Vitamin C.

2. Vitamin E (Tocopherols): Vitamin E is any of several fat soluble vitamins that are chemically tocopherols. Vitamin E is a popular and powerful antioxidant. Vitamin E is effective in preventing the oxidation of polyunsaturated fatty acids. Additionally, Vitamin E is helpful in the prevention of oxidation in the lungs, where strong oxidizing agents nitrogen dioxide and ozone, components of air pollution, are particularly harmful to people exercising. Vitamin E protects white and red blood cells, helping the body's immune system.

3. Calcium (carbonate & citrate): Calcium is essential to many body functions, including the transmission of nerve impulses, the regulation of muscle contraction and relaxation (including of the heart), blood clotting, and various metabolic activities. Calcium is also necessary for maintaining strong bones and is commonly prescribed to prevent and treat postmenopausal osteoporosis (bone thinning). Vitamin D, which aids in the absorption of calcium from the intestine, is often prescribed along with calcium supplements to prevent or treat osteoporosis. (Indeed, some calcium supplement tablets contain vitamin D.)

4. Selenium (sodium selenite): Selenium is a trace mineral that our bodies use to produce

glutathione peroxidase. Glutathione peroxidase is part of the body's antioxidant defense system; it works with vitamin E to protect cell membranes from damage caused by dangerous, naturally occurring substances known as free radicals.

5. Milk Thistle Seed Ext.: Milk Thistle extract promotes healthy, vibrant liver function. The liver is one of the body's most important organs, since it helps rid the body of toxins that can impair good health. The active ingredient in milk thistle thought to give it its beneficial properties is called silymarin. The extract of milk thistle provides a guaranteed potency of 80% silymarin. It is an herb from a plant found in dry rocky soil in Europe and the U.S.

6. Grape seed ext 95%: Grape Seed extract Grape seed extract (GSE) is a bioflavonoid or natural component of most citrus fruits. It is sometimes considered a super-anti-oxidant because its effects as an anti-oxidant are much stronger than other vitamins such as E and C. GSE is also an anti-allergen, anti-histamine and anti-inflammatory. The key feature of GSE is that it strengthens and protects tissues in the body. For this reason, GSE has been used to support healthy cardiovascular, immune and liver (hepatic) systems

7. Schizandra berry is known traditionally for its effects in improving lung, kidney and liver functions by stimulating cells. It is also considered a detoxifying agent as it helps purify the blood and rid the body of toxins. It has also been suggested that schizandra berry improves memory.

8. Psyllium husk: Long known to support general intestinal health, psyllium husk contains a spongy fiber that reduces appetite, improves digestion and cleanses the system.

9. Senna leaf: Also known as Cassia Senna, Senna leaf promotes intestinal and overall health by stimulating elimination and removing solid waste from the body.

10. Pine bark ext 50%: Studies have shown that it has proven beneficial in lowering blood sugar levels in patients suffering from diabetes and help reduce swelling in people with circulation disorders. It has powerful antioxidant components which offer many other benefits as well including protection against arthritis, heart disease, cancers, and diabetes are all on the list of positives. These antioxidant qualities of the pine bark extract may also be key in lowering cholesterol. Antioxidants are also known to support immune system health.

11. Phyllanthus amarus extract: This herb has been used for centuries to support a healthy

immune system and several trials have explored the effects of it on the hepatitis virus with positive results. Plyllanthus amarus extract is also used to support lung health and for overall liver health.

12. Thymus substance: Known for its ability to boost immune health, thymus substance has been used in the treatment of hayfever, asthma, lung infections and food allergies. It is also suggested as part of a wellness plan with AIDS/HIV, arthritis, cancer, herpes and shingles.

13. Bupleurum root: Bupleurum Root is mentioned in Chinese medical texts as long ago ad AD 200. It is considered a remarkable support for a healthy liver, gallbladder and spleen. It botanical compounds also support and nourish digestive system health, as well as natural blood vessel and circulatory health. Bupleurum may also provide herbal support for a healthy nervous system.

14. CoQ10: Coenzyme Q10 (or CoQ10) is a natural chemical compound that we make in our bodies and consume in our diets, primarily from oily fish, organ meats such as liver, and whole grains. CoQ10 can help reduce fatigue, obesity, and a weak immune system (particularly for those with HIV, other viruses, and yeast infections). It also prevents toxin overload, and periodontal.

Early studies show it may also increase sperm motility, leading to enhanced fertility. Several studies suggest that CoQ10 may lower blood pressure after a few weeks, and it might help to prevent some of the heart damage caused by chemotherapy due to it's powerful antioxidant properties.

15. Papain: Made from unripened papaya, papain is supports digestive health and may reduce some types of inflammation.

PROBIOTICS

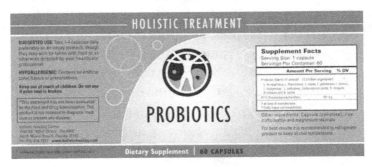

A growing body of scientific evidence suggests that you can treat and even prevent some illnesses with foods and supplements containing certain kinds of live bacteria. Probiotics is designed to replace damaged or dead natural flora in the intestinal track. Many environmental factors, such as poor diet, alcohol and drug use, and exposure to other toxins can damage the intestines and diminish their ability to properly absorb nutrients—a syndrome commonly called leaky gut. Additionally, the absence of the natural flora allows other bacteria and organisms to thrive and can result in candida (yeast) infections and other disorders. Some digestive disease specialists are recommending them for disorders that frustrate conventional medicine, such as irritable bowel syndrome. Since the mid-1990s, clinical studies have established that probiotic therapy may help overcome several gastrointestinal ills and delay the development of allergies. Controlled trials have shown some types of probiotics may shorten the course of diarrhea by 60 percent when compared with a placebo. Probiotic therapy may also help people with Crohn's disease and irritable bowel syndrome. Because of their healing effect on the gastrointestinal system, they are an important supplement in addiction treatment.

To learn more about our nutritional supplements, visit John Giordano 786-271-5732 holisticaddictioninfo.com

For more information and research articles visit http://www.holisticaddictioninfo.com or see the suggested readings section of this book.

OMEGA FATTY ACIDS

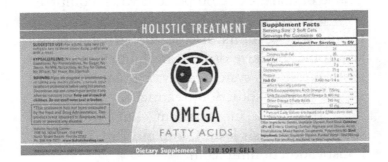

Studies have shown that fish oils with at least 3 grams of EPA and DHA offer significant cardiovascular and digestive benefits. Despite these clinical studies, many fish oil supplements do not supply this level of active ingredient. Our formulation exceeds the recommended dose.

These are the benefits associated with the use of fish oils:

◊   It helps maintain normal cholesterol levels.
◊   It helps maintain normal triglyceride levels.
◊   It promotes healthy blood pressure levels.
◊   It promotes health digestive system.
◊   It helps maintain healthy blood flow.
◊   It support circulatory and vascular health.
◊   It promotes cardiovascular health.
◊   It helps maintain health levels of C-reactive protein.
◊   It promotes healthy complexion.

◊ It enhances mood by promoting healthy brain cell development.

Additional information on the medical benefits of Omega Fatty Acids can be found at http://www.nlm.nih.gov/medlineplus/druginfo/natural/patient-fishoil.html

To learn more about our nutritional supplements, visit John Giordano 786-271-5732 holisticaddictioninfo.com

For more information and research articles visit http://www.holisticaddictioninfo.com or see the suggested readings section of this book.

Most Common Mental Health Disorders Associated with Substance Abuse

BIPOLAR DISORDER

Also known as manic-depressive illness, it is a brain disorder that causes unusual and severe shifts in mood, energy, and ability to function. Different from the normal ups and downs that everyone goes through, the symptoms of bipolar disorder are severe. Bipolar disorder causes dramatic mood swings from overly high and irritable to sad and hopeless and then back again, often with periods of normal mood in between. Severe changes in energy and behavior go along with these changes in mood. The periods of highs and lows are called episodes of mania and depression.

Signs and symptoms of mania (or a manic episode) include:

◊ Increased energy, activity, and restlessness
◊ Excessively high, overly good, euphoric mood
◊ Extreme irritability
◊ Racing thoughts and talking very fast, jumping from one idea to another
◊ Distractibility, can't concentrate well
◊ Little sleep needed
◊ Unrealistic beliefs in one's abilities and powers
◊ Poor judgment
◊ Spending sprees

◊ A lasting period of behavior that is different from usual
◊ Increased sexual drive
◊ Abuse of drugs, particularly cocaine, alcohol, and sleeping medications
◊ Provocative, intrusive, or aggressive behavior
◊ Denial that anything is wrong

Signs and symptoms of depression (or a depressive episode) include:

◊ Lasting sad, anxious, or empty mood
◊ Feelings of hopelessness or pessimism Feelings of guilt, worthlessness, or helplessness
◊ Loss of interest or pleasure in activities once enjoyed, including sex
◊ Decreased energy, a feeling of fatigue or of being slowed down
◊ Difficulty concentrating, remembering, making decisions
◊ Restlessness or irritability
◊ Sleeping too much or can't sleep
◊ Change in appetite and/or unintended weight loss or gain
◊ Chronic pain or other persistent bodily symptoms that are not caused by physical illness or injury

◊ Thoughts of death or suicide or suicide
attempts

Source: www.nimh.nih.gov/publicat/bipolar.cfm

GENERALIZED ANXIETY DISORDER (GAD)

GAD is characterized by six or more months of persistent, exaggerated worry and tension that is unfounded or much more severe than the normal anxiety most people experience. People with these disorders usually expect the worst; they worry excessively about money, health, family, or work even when there are no signs of trouble. They are unable to relax and often suffer from insomnia. Many people with GAD also have physical symptoms, such as fatigue, trembling, muscle tension, headaches, irritability, or hot flashes. GAD often coexists with depression, substance abuse, or other anxiety disorders. Other conditions associated with stress, such as irritable bowel syndrome, often accompany GAD.

Source: www.nimh.nih.gov/Publicat/gad facts.cfm

PANIC DISORDER

Panic disorder is characterized by unexpected and repeated episodes of intense fear accompanied by physical symptoms that may include chest pain, heart palpitations, shortness of breath, dizziness or abdominal distress. These sensations often mimic symptoms of a heart attack or other life-threatening medical conditions. This disorder is often accompanied by phobias about places or situations. Research shows that panic disorder most often coexists with depression and substance abuse. About 30% of people with panic disorder abuse alcohol and 17% abuse drugs, such as cocaine and marijuana, in unsuccessful attempts to alleviate the anguish and distress caused by their condition.

Source: www.nimh.nih.gov/publicat/panic facts.cfm

DEPRESSION

This is a serious medical illness; it's not something that has been made up in your head. It's feeling "down" and "low" and "hopeless" for weeks at a time, most often accompanies substance/ alcohol abuse.

Signs and Symptoms
◊ Persistent sad, anxious, or "empty" mood
◊ Feelings of hopelessness, pessimism
◊ Feelings of guilt, worthlessness, helplessness
◊ Loss of interest or pleasure in hobbies and activities that were once enjoyed

Source: www.nihm.nih.gov/healthinformation/depressionmenu.cfm

ATTENTION DEFICIT HYPERACTIVITY DISORDER (ADHD)

It is one of the most common mental disorders that develop in children. Children with ADHD have impaired functioning in multiple settings, including home, school, and in relationships with peers. If untreated, the disorder can have long-term adverse effects into adolescence and adulthood such as higher rates of injury, depressive, anxiety, and conduct disorders, drug abuse, such as cocaine and methamphetamines, or antisocial behavior.

Signs and Symptoms
◊ Impulsiveness
◊ Hyperactivity, restlessness, fidgety
◊ Inattention, lack of focus
◊ Losing things
◊ Disorganized

Source: www.nimh.nih.gov/HealthInforma tion/adhdmenu.cfm

OBSESSIVE COMPULSIVE DISORDER (OCD)

An anxiety disorder that is characterized by recurrent, unwanted thoughts (obsessions) and/or repetitive behaviors (compulsions). Repetitive behaviors such as hand washing, counting, checking, or cleaning are often performed with the hope of preventing obsessive thoughts or making them go away. Performing these so-called "rituals," however, provides only temporary relief, and not performing them markedly increases anxiety.

Source: www.nimh.nig.gov/HealthInformation/ocdmenu.cfm

POST-TRAUMATIC STRESS DISORDER (PTSD)

An anxiety disorder that can develop after exposure to a terrifying event or ordeal in which grave physical harm occurred or was threatened. Traumatic events that may trigger PTSD include violent personal assaults, natural or human-caused disasters, accidents, or military combat. People with PTSD have persistent frightening thoughts and memories of their ordeal and feel emotionally numb, especially with people they were once close to. They may experience sleep problems, feel detached or numb, or be easily startled. Feelings of intense guilt are also common. Co-occurring depression, alcohol, or other substance abuse, or another anxiety disorders are not uncommon.

Source: www.nimh.nih.gov/publicat/ptsd facts.cfm

RECIPES

Protein Sprinkles

A sprinkle here, a sprinkle there, a nice tasty blend and quick protein punch to add to your salad, toast, rice, avocado, sautéed kale...the list is endless.

½ cup hemp seeds
½ cup nutritional yeast (*Candida albicans*-free)
½ cup sesame seeds
½ tbs. kelp granules
½ tsp. mineral sea salt (optional)

Mix all ingredients together. Store in fridge in a glass jar. For those who have a slower digestive system, you can grind up the hemp seeds and sesame seeds for more absorption. A coffee grinder works well!

SUPER FOOD SALAD

3 cups of cooked quinoa or kaniwa (1c quinoa 2 c water)
1 cup fresh blueberries
1 cup gogi berries
1 cup hemp seeds
1 cup sunflower seed or crushed or walnuts
1 ½ cups of chopped cilantro
1 cup edaname beans shelled & steamed
1 acai smoothie packet or ¾ cup of acai juice
¼ cup coconut oil (liquid consistency & optional)
juice of 2–4 limes
juice of 1–2 oranges

Cook quinoa. Let cool. In a large mixing bowl, add blueberries, sunflower seeds, gogi berries, chopped cilantro and edaname beans. Add coconut oil. Mix the acai smoothie pack in blender with fresh lime and orange juice. Slowly add to salad. Mix together. Eat and enjoy!

POWER PB&F SANDWICH

Who doesn't love a peanut butter and jelly sandwich? Enjoy this healthy upgrade with a delicious power punch. Simple and oh so good!

½ cup peanut butter or nut butter of choice (use nut butters with blood type–specific food chart)
1 slice of ezekiel or gluten-free bread
½ cup sprouts
¼ cup hemp seeds
a handful of sliced strawberries or sliced fresh strawberries or fruit of choice

Toast bread and spread nut butter. Sprinkle some of the hemp seeds on. Add sprouts, then sliced fruit. Sprinkle additional hemp seeds on top. Yum! Enjoy!

Samurai Salmon Burgers

4 cups of cooked short grain brown rice
4 cans of wild salmon or fresh salmon cooked
1 cup chopped cilantro
1 cup crumbled feta cheese (omit or more if you like)
½ to 1 cup ground flax or 1 egg slightly beaten or both
½ cup sautéed onions chopped small
1 cup hemp seeds
½ to 1 cup sunflower seeds (optional)
sea salt to taste
1 tsp. garlic powder
½ tsp. paprika or any spices that you like
grapeseed oil or coconut oil

Mix all ingredients together. Make into burger patties. Refrigerate for about two hours or freeze. Then sauté lightly with some grapeseed or coconut oil. Bon appetit!

This makes about twelve medium burgers.

BRAIN BALLS

1 cup almond butter, peanut butter, or nut butter of your choice
1 cup chopped soaked organic walnuts
1 cup chopped soaked organic almonds
1 cup chopped soaked organic pumpkin seeds
½ cup chia seeds ground
1 cup hemp seeds
1 cup ground gogi berries (optional)
2 tbs. coconut oil
2 tbs. of raw honey
2 tsp. almond extract
1 tsp. sea salt
1 cup shredded coconut

Use soaked nuts if possible (dry well after soaking) or regular organic nuts and seeds. Chop nuts and seeds separately in a small Cuisinart. Grind gogi berries and chia seeds (I use a coffee grinder for these). Mix all ingredients together. Roll into golf-sized balls and roll in coconut. Store in fridge. This will last about two weeks. Enjoy. Yum!

It makes about thirty balls.
Brain food for any time of the day!
Bon appetite!
Happy Eating!

Pati Reiss HHC
The Holistic Gourmet
www.patireiss.com

MORE RECIPE INFO

Pati Reiss HHRC
Holistic health recovery coach and chef

Pati is the founder of High Vibe Recovery Coaching and the Holistic Gourmet, and author of *High Vibe Cookin'* a cookbook for recovery and life! As a recovery coach, she guides clients through a personalized nutrition food plan and helps them set up a daily healthy lifestyle plan that works! Food, amino acid nutrient therapy, cooking skills, and relaxation techniques are the cornerstones of a healthy, happy, and sustainable recovery! Let's eat!

For more information, contact Pati Reis:
www.patiriess.com
Pati@patireiss.com
801-688-2482

TESTAMONIALS

HOLDING OUT FOR A MISDIAGNOSIS

I first picked up when I was fifteen. It didn't take long before I was fully addicted to cocaine. I come from a really nice family, and everybody always did everything they could for me. I don't know what went wrong along the way. I've heard other addicts share that they felt different and less than the others and that some of them had been through really tragic things in their life, but that just wasn't the case with me, or at least I wasn't aware of it at the time.

I didn't know that when I first picked up, it stemmed from not feeling good about myself. I didn't understand that I had a self-esteem problem and that I was always trying to escape from something or feel differently from how I felt by using something outside of myself. No one ever hurt me. No one ever did anything bad things to me—except me.

I continued to use throughout my teenage years, somehow holding things together, mostly because my family was always there to save me. I put on a really good show for everybody for a really long time. I knew that I couldn't live without the drugs, but I didn't get that I was an addict. I suppose I just didn't want to see it, and the drugs certainly helped me see reality the way I wanted to and not the way that it really was.

I thought I was a normal young adult. I honestly thought that doing drugs were just something that all teenagers did. When I moved away from my family to a different state for college, I felt free to be whoever I wanted to be, and the drugs seemed to allow me to do that. It was all an illusion. The drugs made me feel like I could do and be anything. The truth is that I can do and be anything, but not if I'm using drugs. Still, I held up the appearance of success for a while—good schools, great jobs. But it didn't last.

From the time I first picked up, I used consistently. By the time that I got clean, I could not remember having gone one full day clean since I first picked up. Drugs were not the only thing I used—I used people. First, my family and after them, a series of successful men with whom I had unsuccessful relationships. I did not know how to love myself. How could I possibly love another person? As a result of my addiction, I created insanity and dug myself deep into problems that I could not find a way out of alone. It was convenient to have someone around to "save me" and "fix me" and "love me" because I could not take care of or love myself.

The longer I used, the messier things got. I never ended up on the streets, and I never used the needle. But I failed out of school, lost all my good jobs, and destroyed all my relationships. At twenty-three and then a full-blown heroin addict,

I found myself without a home to call my own, alienated from everyone who ever loved me, and lost. And I still did not think I had a problem. I thought this was just a rough spot, and I'd get through it soon enough. It never occurred to me to stop using.

My family members worked together to try to save me one more time, and they did an intervention. I was sent to Holistic. I still did not think that drugs were the problem. I was holding out for a misdiagnosis. I went to treatment to appease my family and because if I did what they wanted, I thought I could get some more money from them after the twenty-eight-day treatment and go back to my old life. I thought that somehow it'd be "better" or "different" this time.

Something happened to me in treatment. I began to understand that my drug problem was merely symptomatic of something much deeper and that my life would never be successful as long as I continued to use. I reluctantly participated in all the activities offered in a complete holistic program, complaining all the way, but nevertheless, I did them.

One day, we went to a ropes course. At this course, they had us do activities where we had to learn to trust ourselves and others. It was scary, but at the same time, it was exhilarating. There was one point where I felt like I couldn't do it, and I tried and failed. But something had me ask to do it again. I succeeded the second time. The feeling that I got from that was so incredible. It was the first real self-esteem, not arrogance or ego, that I felt about myself in a really long time. It has since given me the courage to try things that I failed at before; for example, the staff encouraged me to give college another try. Later this year, I am going to graduate top of my class, and I am enrolling in law school.

During my individual therapy sessions, I learned about setting goals for myself, and I began to do service as well. My therapist encouraged me and empowered me with exercises and assignments. One of the assignments included getting a sponsor and working steps. My sponsor and my therapist worked together and helped me understand that they don't judge me and that I won't get better until I get honest. Maybe I thought I always had to say the right thing or perform a certain way for people to care about me. My therapist at Holistic taught me that I am important and special.

Today, I am clean over two years. I know what honesty is, and I practice it in all my relationships. It's not always easy or comfortable, but even in recovery, I have seen how hurtful and painful dishonesty can be.

Holistic gave me two huge gifts: my self-esteem and encouragement to participate in a twelve-step fellowship. I never would have imagined that I not only could benefit from a twelve-step fellowship but that I really belonged there. I got a sponsor who I know loves me no matter what, and she is my guide through this process of recovering my self-esteem and creating a life that I can be proud of. She is more than just my sponsor, she is my friend.

I have learned how to have relationships with people and my family where they are not built on just bailing me out of trouble all the time. I am someone people can count on now too.

I've heard people say that they have life beyond their wildest dreams in recovery, and I believe that if I keep doing what I learned at Holistic, I will get there too.

—Ali G., recovering addict

LIFE WITH HOPE

Robert Browning once spoke that entertaining hope means recognizing fear. I am beginning to understand how to work through anxiety instead of ignoring it. My spiritual growth has started to blossom in learning to face the actual origin of my problems. In turn, I have allowed my Higher Power to assume responsibility for the things I simply cannot change. When my anxiety tells me there is a problem, I have learned to face it and grow by dealing with it.

I am done living in terror. I felt terror when the drugs ran out and I didn't know how or when to get more. Terror is sitting around, waiting to get dope sick. Terror is being locked in a bathroom for two hours trying to hit and missing the shot. Terror is having an ounce of heroin in the dash and seeing flashing lights approaching. Terror is sticking a need in your arm to live. Terror is hitting rock bottom and knowing that only death or jail could stop me. I lost myself in the abomination and derelict my life had become—a toxic wasteland of my own creation. T. S. Eliot once said that only in my end is my beginning. I have learned to surrender the will that has tormented me on a daily basis.

This program is a course in how to live. One of the most important things that I learned here was how to quiet my mind. The meditation practice courses were key to my new spirituality. But I would never have been able to sit still long enough to know that, however, without the vitamin program. One thing that is really cool is that when I am feeling anxious, there is actually a vitamin to help me with my anxiety. It's not like taking a pill because I know that the product is all natural, and it is helping my body to heal and helping my brain to remember how to relax by itself.

There is also a sleep formula that helped me relax enough and turn the constant thinking off for long enough to finally get some rest. And when I wake up in the morning, there is no hangover or dull feeling. I wake up refreshed and rested. The vitamin therapy and nutraceuticals were an important part of treatment that I didn't get anywhere else. I think they made a huge difference for me.

Because I wasn't so filled with anxiety and run-away thoughts, I was able to pay attention in the group and at the meetings. I received a small MP3 player with some guided meditations to help me. There is a fifteen-minute quick relaxation exercise on the player that I can do anytime or anywhere. We also did meditations and relaxation exercises right before some of the groups. It really helped me and everyone else to relax enough to be able to pay attention and learn something in group. Through the meditations that I am practicing now, I am able to discern between my higher conscious and the lower self that kept me using. I am able to quiet my mind so that I can follow my heart.

I am learning new attitudes toward old problems and new solutions from them by working the steps. Even though I can't change the facts of life, I have begun to learn how to change my attitude toward them.

The last twenty-eight days have been the most important days of my life. This program has illustrated a design of living just for today. No one knows what tomorrow may bring, which is why I choose to live for the present moment. I have learned to give instead of take, to be of service to others as opposed to myself, and most importantly, to let live instead of let die. I have been blessed with the opportunity to seek out the steps, experiences, and knowledge to literally save my life.

This is a disease I bought and paid for. No one called my dealer, put money in my hands, and injected heroin into my veins for me. This is an indiscriminate disease of the soul that no age, sex, or creed can be immune to.

Long before I arrived here, I had doubt in my mind. I had become powerless over my addiction. This honesty led me to hope that a higher power could restore my chaotic existence to sanity. I know if I kept using, I was going to die. I knew every time I stud a needle in my vein or light that pipe, I was becoming days, minutes, and seconds closer to death. I was comfortable with this reality of my existence, and through hell and back I have put myself through, I choose to reclaim sanity in my life. I can no longer blame people, places, and things for my addiction. I must face my problems and feelings. Although we may not be responsible for the onset of our disease, only we have the power to be responsible for our recovery.

I would like to thank everyone here (at G & G Holistic Addiction Treatment) for contributing to my recovery. My newfound peace of mind and self would not be possible without each and every one here. My gratitude is indescribable. The beauty I have seen perpetuate here is unlike any I have ever known. Thank you all for the power to change and for saving my life.

—Gina, recovering addict

My Mom Never Gave Up on Me

I went to sixteen different treatment centers by the time I was twenty years old. I was prescribed Adderall for ADHD when I was six years old. By the time I was fourteen, I had figured out how to get high from my prescription. Around fifteen years old, I began my addiction in earnest with pain pills, cocaine, and marijuana, and in the next few years, I used anything I could get my hands on. At eighteen, I went to my first treatment—I was already using heroin and other opiates. They put me on a maintenance drug to keep me from using street drugs, and I stayed on it for three years. But my cravings had not left, and soon I found crystal meth.

Once I found crystal meth, I was on the streets for good. Every minute of every day was about getting more—*how could I get more?* I did things that I am ashamed of: I stole, I lied, I cheated. I stole from my family the most. I did not care about anyone anymore, especially not myself.

My family—especially my mom—never gave up on me. She just kept finding me and sending me to another treatment center, always hoping that this one would be where I would get the help I needed to get better. I remember one year where I was kicked out or where I ran away from so many places that I was in a different treatment center every sixty days. It just seemed like nothing was going to work for me.

I got arrested several times. But when I finally violated probation for the fourth time, there was nothing that a new lawyer or my family would be able to do to save me if I messed up again. I can't say I was ready, I wasn't. I can't even say that I wanted to stop using yet. I only wished that I really wanted to stop using.

The holistic approach made a huge difference for me. The holistic testing wasn't just a bunch of questions. They drew my blood, checked my urine, and even tested a sample of my hair. The tests were a complete biochemical profile to see what systems in my body weren't working well, what nutrients I needed more of, and which I had too much of as well. The hair analysis even included a test for heavy metal poisoning like lead and mercury.

As it turned out, I had super high levels of heavy metal that were making my ADHD worse. No wonder I couldn't sit through a meeting or a group therapy. It was such a relief to learn that it wasn't my fault, that there was a reason that I couldn't pay attention or sit still, and it wasn't just that I was lazy.

I started taking nutraceuticals and vitamins to help heal my brain. And I began using the mild hyperbaric oxygen therapy (HBOT). The combination of those two things made a huge difference for me. Before, it was like always seeing everything through a dirty window. The vitamins plus HBOT cleaned the window so that I can see and think clearly. That's what detoxifying and healing my brain using the nutriceutical program and the HBOT has been like for me.

Today, I not only can sit through a sixty-minute meeting, I am the chairperson of a meeting once a week. I am interning at the treatment center, and I still do all the therapies and treatments there. My life is totally different now. I am able to set and achieve goals, and I do not crave drugs all the time. I actually don't want to use anymore. How miraculous is that!

—Michael H., recovering addict

PAIN AND PILLS

When I was nine years old, I began having really bad headaches. They were diagnosed as migraines, and I was given pain medication for them.

In high school, I began to drink and smoke pot secretly in my closet before school. Not even my friends knew. Throughout the rest of my teens, I experimented with other drugs, but none of them really held my attention. There was always this underlying desire to escape. I just felt empty inside.

It all really started for me at six years old when the dentist gave me nitrous oxide, and I remember thinking, "I always want to feel this good." Around ten or eleven years old, I was sneaking into my mother's cabinet to steal my pain pills even when I didn't need them.

By twenty-three, I was married and I was pregnant and so hopeful about the future. Something went wrong, and the baby was stillborn. I was given pain medication for the C-section, and at her funeral I never cried. I felt nothing because I was so doped up. A few years later, I was diagnosed with lupus. Again, legitimate pain pills for my legitimate pain.

But the emptiness was always there, and it grew deeper and darker. More and more, I turned to the pain medication to help me through the day, always thinking, *Tomorrow I won't take any. Tomorrow will be a better day.*

Finally, I decided to go to treatment. Nothing really bad had happened. I never got arrested, I didn't overdose. My family didn't even realize that I had a problem. But I knew that I couldn't go on the way I was living.

Something that really helped me during treatment and even to this day, almost four years later, are the music and meditation downloads that is used in treatment. This technology literally tapped into something deep inside of me, sort of woke it up. And this was exactly what I needed to stop feeling so empty inside.

I use this technology every day. I find that listening to the meditation or the subliminal recordings helps me stay centered and relaxed throughout my day. This technology has helped me discover a peace and serenity that I never thought possible.

I have been able to learn alternative ways to manage the pain of lupus. Learning how to relax and using the guided meditations have helped tremendously. Honestly, I don't have pain like I did when I was using. I feel good, and I feel good about myself.

—Marcy U., recovering addict

AWAKENING

My name is George, and I'm a fifty-nine-year-old black male college graduate and father of two boys, who has a severe problem with drugs and alcohol. My problem was active for thirty years—so that means I was part of sixties generation and participated in Woodstock and experimented with all the drugs that went with that lifestyle.

Ultimately, I got involved with heroin. Then I began first snorting coke then smoking crack. All the while, I was pretending that I was a responsible dad, responsible employee, and wonderful husband. None of that was the truth. I lived a "Jekyll and Hyde" existence.

Both of my children played hockey, baseball, etc., and I was often a coach for their teams. I was always there, but never present. I was either hung over or planning on doing something that would lead to a hang over.

At one point, my wife, a professor a Syracuse, threatened to divorce me if I did not go to treatment. That led me to my first treatment episode. It was a wonderful program in New York, but it failed to bring out the best in me. It was a lockdown facility where my ability to interact with my family and the world at large was severely limited. It was like being a prisoner.

Two days after leaving treatment, I was drinking again, and a week later, I was using cocaine again.

These behaviors ultimately led to my wife divorcing me, and I became separated from my family. That was devastating to me, but of course, I used drugs and alcohol to self-medicate and sooth my emotional wounds.

I found G & G Holistic Addiction Treatment in Florida through the parents of another hockey player on my son's team. They had experience with several treatment programs and Holistic was where they had finally achieved success: long-term abstinence.

My family insisted I was as bad as he was and that if he could be cured at G & G, so could I. I was soon on my way to North Miami Beach and G & G.

I was extremely surprised with the approach: the vitamins, the gym, yoga, karate. We went to the store, and we went to outside meetings. I was not barred from interacting with the world; in fact, it was encouraged. We kept our cell phones and were allowed computer access even. The entire milieu was real-world based. It was a far cry from the imprisonment of previous treatment.

I was a practicing Quaker who had lost sight of my spiritual side during active addiction. At G & G, I was encouraged to rediscover my relationship with a Higher Power through meditation. I was able to reconnect with that which created and rules the universe.

During the course of my stay, I had a primary therapist who gave me the opportunity and prompting to experience the miracle of myself and my life. I also became an active member of the fellowship of Alcoholics Anonymous.

I am grateful to have been able to recapture my life and understand the importance to responsible thinking. I now enjoy the opportunity to give back. I work in the field of addiction, and I believe I have found my calling.

—George S., recovering alcoholic

Defining Myself

In the years prior to coming to Holistic, I couldn't stay clean for more than nine months. I was a chronic relapser. Once, since I first started drinking and drugging, I had a period of sobriety that lasted about four years, but that was many years ago, in my early twenties.

My basic issue and problem before I got to Holistic was that I had no idea who I was. I was living into perfect ideals and just kind of wandering. I really couldn't stand myself.

I had been a therapist since 2000 and worked in hospice doing family therapy and counseling. Holistic was the fifth treatment center that I went to. No other treatment taught me the spiritual principles, and no one had ever tried to help me discover who I really am as a person.

I had to learn that my thinking and my perception were off. Even then, since I was a little girl, my emotions were off. I was always so sensitive, especially as a child. I had all these emotions and feelings, and I was in a family of perfectionists. I never understood why I wasn't perfect like the rest of my family was and like how they expected me to be.

I was an athlete, and I was really good. I played on the professional circuit. I ended up at my first treatment center at twenty-one years old, the same year that I retired from professional sports. When I stopped playing my sport, I no longer knew who I was as a person. And I was angry because my career had ended so early.

At Holistic, I learned about authenticity. I learned that the real me is below the surface. I had always depended on what others saw of me, what others thought of me, and how I performed to define myself. I was a human *doing* not a human *being*. Through the spiritual education and instruction that I got at Holistic, I was able to reconnect with what created me. That same Power knows me and has helped me begin to define myself.

I don't think that I ever had the unique spirituality that I got at Holistic. I had heard the saying that I was a spiritual being, and it resonated with me, but I never knew what it meant. Holistic opened the door for me to experience myself as a spiritual being. And through that, I was able to start letting go of the past.

I am now able to enjoy my athleticism again without being mad that my career in athletics is over. I have always enjoyed exercising and athletics. You could say that they are what I know. During treatment, I was able to get back into the gym for the first time in a long time. I am several years clean now, and I still work out every day.

At first, going to the gym was something to do. It kept me busy, and it kept me from gaining too much weight in the beginning of my recovery.

Now, walking on the treadmill is my antistress therapy. It helps me wind down at the end of the day. It gives me time to do some reading. It keeps me from isolating and helps me meet new people. It also supports my health and fitness goals.

—Shea H., recovering alcoholic

Glossary

twelve-steps—a guide to help alcoholics/addicts/ gamblers and food addicts to acquire a new way of life.

AA—Alcoholics Anonymous, a self-help group of recovering alcoholics.

Al-Anon—A self-help group for families of alcoholics.

dual diagnoses—person who has two different disorders coexisting (existing at the same time) such as substance abuse and mental health disorders.

GA—Gamblers Anonymous, a self-help group for recovering gamblers.

NA—Narcotics Anonymous, a self-help group of recovering drug addicts.

Nar-Anon—A self-help group for families of addicts.

OA—Overeaters Anonymous, a self-help group for overeaters.

sponsor—a person who guides you through the twelve-steps. A person you can learn to have a healthy relationship with. Not based on sex, but on trust, understanding, and communication. It's based on one addict helping another.

OUR PUBLICATIONS

Neuro-Psychopharmacogenetics and Neurological Antecedents of Post-traumatic Stress Disorder: Unlocking the Mysteries of Resilience and Vulnerability.Bowirrat A, Chen TJ, Blum K, Madigan M, Bailey JA, Chuan Chen AL, Downs BW, Braverman ER, Radi S, Waite RL, Kerner M, Giordano J, Morse S, Oscar-Berman M, Gold M.Curr Neuropharmacol. 2010 Dec; 8 (4):335–58.

Healing enhancement of chronic venous stasis ulcers utilizing H-WAVE(R) device therapy: a case series. Blum K, Chen AL, Chen TJ, Downs BW, Braverman ER, Kerner M, Savarimuthu S, Bajaj A, Madigan M, Blum SH, Reinl G, Giordano J, Dinubile N.Cases J. 2010 Feb 10;3:54.

Neurogenetics of dopaminergic receptor supersensitivity in activation of brain reward circuitry and relapse: proposing "deprivation-amplification relapse therapy" (DART). Blum K, Chen TJ, Downs BW, Bowirrat A, Waite RL, Braverman ER, Madigan M, Oscar-Berman M, DiNubile N, Stice E, Giordano J, Morse S, Gold M. 2009.

Do dopaminergic gene polymorphisms affect mesolimbic reward activation of music listening response? Therapeutic impact on Reward Deficiency Syndrome (RDS). Blum K, Chen TJ, Chen AL, Madigan M, Downs BW, Waite RL, Braverman ER, Kerner M, Bowirrat A, Giordano J, Henshaw H, Gold MS. Med Hypotheses. 2010 Mar;74(3):513–20. Epub 2009 Nov 14.

Genetic Addiction Risk Score (Gars) Analysis: Exploratory Development of Polymorphic risk Alleles in Polydrug addicted males. Blum k, Giordano j, Morse S, Liu Y, Tain J, Bowirrat A, Smolen A, Waite R, Down B, Madigan M, Kerner M, Fornari F, Barverman E, Miller D, Bailey J. IIOAB Vol1 (20 1–14.)

Neurogenetics and clinical evidence for the putative activation of the brain reward circuitry by a neuroadaptagen: proposing an addiction candidate gene panel map. J Chen TJ, Blum K, Chen AL, Bowirrat A, Downs WB, Madigan MA, Waite RL, Bailey JA, Kerner M, Yeldandi S, Majmundar N, Giordano J, Morse S, Miller D, Fornari F, Braverman ER. Psychoactive Drugs. 2011 Apr-Jun; 43(2):108–27.

Test of variables of attention (TOVA) as a predictor of early attention complaints, an antecedent to dementia. Braverman ER,

Chen AL, Chen TJ, Schoolfield JD, Notaro A, Braverman D, Kerner M, Blum SH, Arcuri V, Varshavskiy M, Damle U, Downs BW, Waite RL, Oscar-Berman M, Giordano J, Blum K. Neuropsychiatr Dis Treat. 2010 Oct 15; 6:681–90.

Overcoming qEEG abnormalities and reward gene deficits during protracted abstinence in male psychostimulant and polydrug abusers utilizing putative dopamine D? agonist therapy: part 2. Blum K, Chen TJ, Morse S, Giordano J, Chen AL, Thompson J, Allen C, Smolen A, Lubar J, Stice E, Downs BW, Waite RL, Madigan MA, Kerner M, Fornari F, Braverman ER.Postgrad Med. 2010 Nov; 122(6):214–26.

Understanding the high mind Humans are still evolving genetically. Blum K, Giordano J, Morse S, Bowirrat A, Madigan M, Downs W, Waite R, Kerner M, Damle U, Braverman ER, Bauer G, Femino J, Bailey J, Dinunile N, Miller D, Archer T, Simpatico T. The IIOAB Journal ISSN: 0976-3104 IIOAB-India Vol. 1; Issue 2; 2010 1–14.

Hypothesizing Synergy between Acupuncture/ Auriculotherapy and Natural Activation of Mesolimbic Dopaminergic Pathways: Putative Natural Treatment Modalities for the Reduction of Drug Hunger and Relapse. Kenneth Blum, John Giordano, Siobhan Morse, Arthur Anderson, Javier Carbajal, Roger Waite, Bernarld Downs, Jaclyn Downs, Margaret Madigan, Debmalya Barh, Eric Braverman IIOAB Letters Vol 1, No 1 (2011)

Genetic Addiction Risk Score(GARS): Testing for Polygentic Predisposition and Risk for Reward Deficiency Syndrome (RDS). Blum K, Fornari F, Downs BW, Waite RL, Giordano J, Smolen A, Lui Y, Tain J, Majmundr N, Braverman ER. Chapter 19: in Gene Therapy Applications (Ed. C King) pages 327–362.

Correlation of the Taq1 Dopamine D2 Receptor Gene and Percent Body Fat in Obese and Screened Control Subjects: A Preliminary Report." Chen Alc, Blu K, Chen TJH, Giordano J, Downs BW, Han D., Barh D., Braverman. Journal of Food & Function (J Royal Society of Chemistry) in press.

Can the chronic administration of the combination of buprenorphine and naloxone block doaminergic activity causing anti-reward and relapse potential? Blum K, Chen TJh, Bailey J, Bowirrat A., Femino J, Chen ALC, Simpatico T, Morse S., Giordano J., Damle U, Kerner M, Braverman Er, Fornari F, Downs

BW, Rector C, Barh D, Oscar-Berman M. Journal of Molecular Neurobiology (in Press).

The Marc ProTM Device Improves Muscle Performance and Recovery From Concentric and Eccentric Exercise Induced Muscle Fatigue In Humans: A Pilot Study. Wayne L. Westcott, PhD, Thomas JH Chen, Gary Reinl, Nicholas Dinubile, MD, Abdalla Bowirrat,MD.,PhD, Margaret Madigan BSN, B. William Downs, B.Sc., John Giordano, MAC, PhD (Hon), Siobhan Morse, MHSA,Anish Bajaj DC, Eric Braverman, MD, Max Blakemore BS, Scott Whitehead,BA, Francis B Neric, MS, CSCS, Lester Sacks,MD,PhD, Kenneth Blum, PhD. Journal of Exercise Physiology Online. 2011 Apr 14 (2), 55–67.

Exercise and Nutrition More Effective than Exercise Alone for Increasing Lean Weight and Reducing Resting Blood Pressure. WestcottW, Varghesse J, Dinubile N, Moynih N, Loud RL, Whitehead S, Brothers S, Giordano J, Morse S, Madigan M, Blum K. Journal of Exercise Physiologistsonline. 2011Aug 14 (4), 120–133.

MarcProTM Device a Novel Paradigm Shift in Muscle Conditioning, Recovery And Performance: Induction of Nitric Oxide

(NO) Dependent Enhanced Microcirculation Coupled with Angiogenesis Mechanisms. Dinubile N, Westcott W, Reinl G, Balai A, Braverman ER, Madigan M, Giordano J, Blum K. Journal of Exercise Physiologistsonline Journal of Exercise Physiology Online. 2011 Oct 14 (5) 10–19.

Neuro-Genetics of Reward Deficiency Syndrome (Rds) as the Root Cause of "Addiction Transfer": A New Phenomena Common after Bariatric Surgery. Kenneth Blum, John Bailey, Anthony Gonzales, Marlene–Oscar-Berman, Yijun Liu1, John Giordano, Eric Braverman and Mark Gold. Genet Syndr Gene Ther 2011, S:2

Generational Association Studies of Dopaminergic Genes in Reward Deficiency Syndrome (RDS) Subjects: Selecting Appropriate Phenotypes for Reward Dependence Behaviors. Kenneth Blum Amanda LC Chen, Marlene Oscar-Berman, Thomas JH Chen, Joel Lubar, Nancy White, Judith Lubar, Abdalla Bowirrat, Eric Braverman, John Schoolfield, Roger L Waite, Bernard W Downs, Margaret Madigan, David E Comings, Caroline Davis, Mallory M Kerner, Jennifer Knopf, Tomas Palomo, John J. Giordano, Siobhan A. Morse, Frank Fornari, Debmalya Barh, John Femino and John A Bailey. Int. J. Environ. Res. Public Health 2011.

Nutrigenomics of Neuradaptogen Amino-Acid-Therapy (NAAT): Overcoming Carbohydrate Bingeing and Overeating Through Neurometabolic Mechanisms. Blum K, Bagchi, D., Bowirrat A, Downs BW, Waite RL, Giordano J, Morse S, Madigan M, Downs JM, Braverman ER, Polanin M, Simpatico T Functional Foods in Health and Disease, 2011

Early Intervention of Intravenous KB220IV-Neuroadaptagen Amino-Acid Therapy (NAAT)" Improves Behavioral Outcomes in a Residential Addiction Treatment Program: A Pilot Study. Miller M, , Chen ALC, Stokes S, Silverman S, Manka M, Manka D, Miller D, Perrine K, Chen TJH, Bailey J, Downs BW, Damle U, Waite RL, Madigan M, Braverman, Kerner M, Giordano J, Oscar-Berman M, Blum K. J Psychoactive Drugs (in Press).

Depressed Dopamine Function in Attention Deficit/Hyperactivity Disorder (ADHD): Should Genotyping of Dopaminergic and Other Gene Polymorphisms Constitute Early Diagnosis in Children? Blum K, Tucker D, Graham NA, Bailey J, Bowirrat A, Barh D, Giordano J, Braverman ER, Oscar-Berman

M, Gold M. BMC-Advances in Integrative Omics and Applied Biotechnology: Review & Hypothesis9 (In Press).

Hypothesizing Reward Deficiency Syndrome (RDS) as the root cause of "addiction transfer": A new phenomena common after bariatric surgery. Blum K, Bailey J, Gonzales A, Liu Y, Stice E, Giordano J., Braverman E, Downs BW, Gold M. Obesity Surg (in review)

Diagnosis and Healing in Veterans Suspected of Suffering From Post-traumatic Stress Disorder (PTSD) Using Reward Gene Testing and Reward Circuitry Natural Dopaminergic Activation. Blum k, Bailey J, Giordano J, Borsten J, Waite RL, Downs BW, Downs JM, Madigan M, Fornarii F., Simpatico T, Jones D, Braverman, Barh D. Canadian Medical Journal (in review).

Audio Therapy Significantly Attenuates Aberrant Mood in Residential Patient Addiction Treatment: Putative Activation of Dopaminergic Pathways in the Meso-Limbic Reward Circuitry of Humans. Morse S, Giordano J, Perrine K, Downs BW, Waite RL, Madigan M, Bailey J, Braverman, Damle U, Simpatico T, Moelelr MD, Blum K. Journal of Addiction Therapy (in review)

Neuropsychiatric Genetics of Happiness, Friendships and Politics: Hypothesizing that "Birds of a Feather (Homophily)" Flock Together as a Function of "Reward Gene (s)" Polymorphisms. Blum K, Oscar-Berman M, Bowirrat A, Giordano J, Madigan M, Braverman Er, Fornari F. Journal Political Science (submitted)

Neuropsychopharmacology and Neurogenetic Aspects of Executive Functioning: Are Humans "Hard Wired" To Achieve Appropriate Goals? Bowirrat A, Amanda LCH, Madigan M, Chen TJH, Bailey J, Braverman ER, Kerner M, Giordano J, Morse S, Downs BW, Waite RL, Oscar Berman M, Blum K. Neuroscience Research (Submitted)

Quantitative Electroencephalography Analysis (qEEG) of Neuro-Electro-Adaptive Therapy 12" [NEAT12] Up-Regulates Cortical Potentials in an Alcoholic During Protracted Abstinence: Putative Anti-Craving Implications.

Waite RL, Allen C, Giordano J, Morse S, Bowirrat A, Downs BW, Madigan M, Braverman ER, Kerner M, Bailey J, Blum K. BMC-Journal of Medical Case Reports (in review)

Selecting Appropriate Phenotypes for Reward Dependence Behaviors. Blum k, Chen

311

ALCH, Chen TJH, Lubar J, White N, Lubar J, Bowirrat A, Braverman ER, Scholfield J, Waite RL, Downs BW, Madigan M, Comings DE, Davis C Kerner M, Palomo T, Stice E, Oscar-Berman M, Giordano J, Morse S, Bailey J. International Journal of environmental Research and Public Health (in review)

H-Wave Device Augments Healing by Inducing Cellular Mechanisms Responsible For Increased Blood Flow and Loading of Injured Tissue: A hypothesis Having implications for Clinical Practice. Blum k, Chen TJH, Reinl G, Chen ALCH, Dinubile N, Madigan M, Downs BW, Bowirrat A, Bajaj A, Morse S, Giordano J, Westcott W, Smith L, Kerner M, Damle U, Barverman ER, Sacks L. BMC-Skeletal Muscle Disorders (submitted)

Withdrawal associated with buprenorphine/ naloxone (Suboxone) and evidence for a natural dopaminergic agonist [KB220Z] opioid substitution maintenance adjunct: A case report. Blum K, Chen ALCH, Oscar-Berman M, Waite RL, Benya L, Chen TJH, Giordano J, Borste J, Downs BW, Madigan M, Braverman ER, Simpatico T, Fornari F, Barh D, Bailey J. Biological Psychiatry (to be submitted).

Neuropsychopharmacology and Neurogenetic Aspects of Executive Functioning: Should Reward Gene Polymorphisms Constitute a Diagnostic Tool to Identify Individuals at Risk for Impaired Judgment ? Bowirrat AB, Oscar-Berman-M, Madigan M, Bailey J, Bravrman ER, Giordano J, Morse S, Downs BW, Waite R, Fornari F, Blum K. Revised submitted to Molecular Neurobiology (should be accepted soon).

Sex, Drugs, and Rock 'n' Roll: Hypothesizing Common Mesolimbic Activation as a Function of Reward Gene Polymorphisms. Blum K, Werner T, Carnes S, Carnes P, Bowirrat AB, Giordano J, Oscar-Berman M, Gold M. Journal Psychoactive Drugs. (in Press) 2012

The Addictive Brain : All Roads Lead to Dopamine. Blum, K., Chen, LC., Giordano, J., Borsten, J., Chen, T., JH., Hauser, M., Simpatico, T., Femino, J., Braverman, E. R., Barh, D. Journal Psychoactive Drugs. 2012

For a continually updated list of our publications and to view videos please visit http://www. holisticaddictioninfo.com

BIBLIOGRAPHY AND SUGGESTED READINGS

Alcoholics Anonymous. *Alcoholics Anonymous.* 4th ed. New York, NY: A. A. World Services, 2001.

Amen, D. and Smith, D. *Unchain Your Brain.* CA: MindWork Press, 2010.

Beattie, M. *Codependent No More: How to Stop Controlling Others and Start Caring for Yourself.* Center City, MN: Hazeldon

Blum, K., A. L. Chen, T. J. Chen, B. W. Downs, E. R. Braverman, M. Kerner, S. Savarimuthu, A. Bajaj, M. Madigan, S. H. Blum, G. Reinl, J. Giordano, and N. Dinubile. "Healing enhancement of chronic venous stasis ulcers utilizing H-WAVE(R) device therapy: a case series." *Cases Journal* 3, no. 54 (2010).

Blum, K., T. J. Chen, B. W. Downs, A. Bowirrat, R. L. Waite, E. R. Braverman, M. Madigan, M. Oscar-Berman, N. DiNubile, E. Stice, J. Giordano, S. Morse, and M. Gold. "Neurogenetics of Dopaminergic Receptor Supersensitivity in Activation of Brain Reward Circuitry and Relapse: Proposing

"Deprivation-Amplification Relapse Therapy (DART)." *Postgraduate Medicine* 121, no. 6 (2009): 176–96.

Blum, K., T. J. Chen, A. L. Chen, M. Madigan, B. W. Downs, R. L. Waite, E. R. Braverman, M. Kerner, A. Bowirrat, J. Giordano, H. Henshaw, and M. S. Gold. "Do Dopaminergic Gene Polymorphisms Affect Mesolimbic Reward Activation of Music Listening Response? Therapeutic Impact on Reward Deficiency Syndrome (RDS)." *Medical Hypotheses* 74, no. 3 (2010): 513–20.

Blum, K., J. Giordano, S. Morse, Y. Liu, J. Tain, A. Bowirrat, A. Smolen, R. Waite, B. Down, M. Madigan, M. Kerner, F. Fornari, E. Barverman, D. Miller, and J. Bailey. "Genetic Addiction Risk Score (Gars) Analysis: Exploratory Development of Polymorphic Risk Alleles in Polydrug Addicted Males." *IIOAB* 1 no. 2 (2010): 1–14.

Blum, K., T. J. Chen, J. Bailey, A. Bowirrat, J. Femino, A. L. Chen, T. Simpatico, S. Morse, J. Giordano, U. Damle, M. Kerner, E. Braverman, F. Fornari, B. W. Downs, C. Rector, D. Barh, and M. Oscar-Berman. "Can the Chronic Administration of the Combination of Buprenorphine and Naloxone Block Doaminergic Activity Causing Anti-Reward and Relapse Potential?" *Mol Neurobiol* 44 no. 3 (2011): 250–68.

Blum, K., M. Oscar-Berman, A. Bowirrat, J. Giordano, M. Madigan, E. R. Braverman, and F. Fornari. "Neuropsychiatric Genetics of Happiness, Friendships and Politics: Hypothesizing that "Birds of a Feather (Homophily)" Flock Together as a Function of "Reward Gene (s)" Polymorphisms." *Journal Political Science*. Submitted.

Blum, K., A. L. C. Chen, T. J. Chen, J. Lubar, N. White, J. Lubar, A. Bowirrat, E. R. Braverman, J. Scholfield, R. L. Waite, B. W. Downs, M. Madigan, D. E. Comings, C. Davis, M. Kerner, T. Palomo, E. Stice, M. Oscar-Berman, J. Giordano, S. Morse, and J. Bailey. "Selecting Appropriate Phenotypes for Reward Dependence Behaviors." *International Journal of Environmental Research and Public Health*. In review.

Blum, K., T. J. Chen, G. Reinl, A. L. Chen, N. Dinubile, M. Madigan, B. W. Downs, A. Bowirrat, A. Bajaj, S. Morse, J. Giordano, W. Westcott, L. Smith, M. Kerner, U. Damle, E. R. Barverman, and L. Sacks. "H-Wave Device Augments Healing by Inducing Cellular Mechanisms Responsible for Increased Blood Flow and Loading of Injured Tissue: A

Hypothesis Having Implications for Clinical Practice." *Skeletal Muscle Disorders*. Submitted.

Blum, K., A. L. Chen, M. Oscar-Berman, R. L. Waite, L. Benyam, T. J. Chen, J. Giordano, J. Borste, B. W. Downs, M. Madigan, E. R. Braverman, T. Simpatico, F. Fornari, D. Barh, and J. Bailey. "Withdrawal Associated with Buprenorphine/Naloxone (Suboxone) and Evidence for a Natural Dopaminergic Agonist [KB220Z] Opioid Substitution Maintenance Adjunct: A Case Report." *Biological Psychiatry*. To be submitted.

Blum, K., T. Werner, S. Carnes, P. Carnes, A. B. Bowirrat, J. Giordano, M. Oscar-Berman, and M. Gold. "Sex, Drugs, and Rock 'n' Roll: Hypothesizing Common Mesolimbic Activation as a Function of Reward Gene Polymorphisms." *Journal Psychoactive Drugs*. In press. 2012.

Blum, K., D. Tucker, N. A. Graham, J. Bailey, A. Bowirrat, D. Barh, J. Giordano, E. R. Braverman, M. Oscar-Berman, and M. Gold. "Depressed Dopamine Function in Attention Deficit/Hyperactivity Disorder (ADHD): Should Genotyping of Dopaminergic and Other Gene Polymorphisms Constitute Early Diagnosis in Children?" *Advances in*

Integrative Omics and Applied Biotechnology. In press. 2012.

Blum, K., J. Bailey, A. Gonzales, Y. Liu, E. Stice, J. Giordano, E. Braverman, B. W. Downs, and M. Gold. "Hypothesizing Reward Deficiency Syndrome (RDS) as the Root Cause of 'Addiction transfer': A New Phenomena Common after Bariatric Surgery." *Obesity Surg.* In review.

Blum, K., J. Bailey, J. Giordano, J. Borsten, R. L. Waite, B. W. Downs, J. M. Downs, M. Madigan, F. Fornarii, T. Simpatico, D. Jones, E. R. Braverman, and D. Barh. "Diagnosis and Healing in Veterans Suspected of Suffering from Post-Traumatic Stress Disorder (PTSD) Using Reward Gene Testing and Reward Circuitry Natural Dopaminergic Activation." *Canadian Medical Journal.* In review.

Blum, K., T. J. Chen, S. Morse, J. Giordano, A. L. Chen, J. Thompson, C. Allen, A. Smolen, J. Lubar, E. Stice, B. W. Downs, R. L. Waite, M. A. Madigan, M. Kerner, F. Fornari, and E. R. Braverman. "Overcoming qEEG Abnormalities and Reward Gene Deficits during Protracted Abstinence in Male Psychostimulant and Polydrug Abusers Utilizing Putative Dopamine D? Agonist

Therapy: Part 2." *Postgrad Med.* Nov. 122 no. 6 (2010): 214–26.

Blum, K., L. C. Chen, J. Giordano, J. Borsten, T. J. H.Chen, M. Hauser, T. Simpatico, J. Femino, E. R. Braverman, D. Barh. "The Addictive Brain: All Roads Lead to Dopamine." *Journal Psychoactive Drugs* 44 no. 2 (2012): 134–43.

Blum, K., J. Bailey, A. Gonzales, M. Oscar-Berman, Y. Yijun Liu, J. Giordano, E. Braverman, and M. Gold. "Neuro-Genetics of Reward Deficiency Syndrome (Rds) as the Root Cause of 'Addiction Transfer': A New Phenomena Common after Bariatric Surgery." *Genet Syndr Gene Ther*, S:2 (2011).

Blum, K., A. L. C. Chen, M. Oscar-Berman, T. J. H. Chen, J. Lubar, N. White, J. Lubar, A. Bowirrat, E. Braverman, J. Schoolfield, R. L. Waite, B. W. Downs, M. Madigan, D. E. Comings, C. Davis, M. M. Kerner, J. Knopf, T. Palomo, J. J. Giordano, S. A. Morse, F. Fornari, D. Barh, J. Femino, and J. A. Bailey. "Generational Association Studies of Dopaminergic Genes in Reward Deficiency Syndrome (RDS) Subjects: Selecting Appropriate Phenotypes for Reward Dependence Behaviors." *Int. J. Environ. Res. Public Health* 8 no. 12(2011): 4425–59.

Blum, K., D. Bagchi, A. Bowirrat, B. W. Downs, R. L. Waite, J. Giordano, S. Morse, M. Madigan, J. M. Downs, E. R. Braverman, M. Polanin, T. Simpatico. "Nutrigenomics of Neuradaptogen Amino-Acid-Therapy: Overcoming Carbohydrate Bingeing and Overeating Through Neurometabolic Mechanisms." *Functional Foods in Health and Disease* 9, 310–78.

Blum, K., J. Giordano, S. Morse, A. Bowirrat, M. Madigan, W. Downs, R. Waite, M. Kerner, U. Damle, E. R. Braverman, G. Bauer, J. Femino, J. Bailey, N. Dinunile, D. Miller, T. Archer, and T. Simpatico. "Understanding the High Mind Humans Are Still Evolving Genetically." *IIOAB* 1 no. 2 (2010): 1–14.

Blum, K., J. Giordano, S. Morse, A. Anderson, J. Carbajal, R. Waite, B. Downs, J. Downs, M. Madigan, D. Barh, and E. Braverman. "Hypothesizing Synergy between Acupuncture/ Auriculotherapy and Natural Activation of Mesolimbic Dopaminergic Pathways: Putative Natural Treatment Modalities for the Reduction of Drug Hunger and Relapse." *IIOAB Letters* 1 no. 1 (2011): 8–20.

Blum, K., F. Fornari, B. W. Downs, R. L. Waite, J. Giordano, A. Smolen, Y. Lui, J. Tain, N.

Majmundr, and E. R. Braverman. "Genetic Addiction Risk Score (GARS): Testing for Polygentic Predisposition and Risk for Reward Deficiency Syndrome (RDS)," in C. Kang (Ed.) *Gene Therapy Applications*. Rijeka, Croatia: InTech, 2011.

Bowirrat, A., L. C. Amanda, M. Madigan, T. J. Chen, J. Bailey, E. R. Braverman, M. Kerner, J. Giordano, S. Morse, B. W. Downs, R. L. Waite, M. Oscar-Berman, and K. Blum. "Neuropsychopharmacology and Neurogenetic Aspects of Executive Functioning: Are Humans 'Hard Wired' to Achieve Appropriate Goals?" *Neuroscience Research*. Submitted.

Bowirrat, A. B., M. Oscar-Berman, M. Madigan, J. Bailey, E. R. Bravrman, J. Giordano, S. Morse, B. W. Downs, R. Waite, F. Fornari, and K. Blum. "Neuropsychopharmacology and Neurogenetic Aspects of Executive Functioning: Should Reward Gene Polymorphisms Constitute a Diagnostic Tool to Identify Individuals at Risk for Impaired Judgment?" Revised submitted to *Molecular Neurobiology*—should be accepted soon.

Bowirrat, A., T. J. Chen, K. Blum, M. Madigan, J. A. Bailey, C. A. L. Chuan, B. W. Downs, E. R. Braverman, S. Radi, R. L. Waite, M. Kerner, J.

Giordano, S. Morse, M. Oscar-Berman, and M. Gold. "Neuro-Psychopharmacogenetics and Neurological Antecedents of Post-Traumatic Stress Disorder: Unlocking the Mysteries of Resilience and Vulnerability." *Curr Neuropharmacol.* Dec. 8 no. 4 (2010): 335–58.

Braverman, E. R., A. L. Chen, T. J. Chen, J. D. Schoolfield, A. Notaro, D. Braverman, M. Kerner, S. H. Blum, V. Arcuri, M. Varshavskiy, U. Damle, B. W. Downs, R. L. Waite, M. Oscar-Berman, J. Giordano, and K. Blum. "Test of Variables of Attention (TOVA) as a Predictor of Early Attention Complaints, an Antecedent to Dementia." *Neuropsychiatr Dis Treat* 6 no. 1 (2010): 681–90.

Cass, H. and K. Barnes. *8 Weeks to Vibrant Health.* Brevard, NC: Take Charge Books, 2008.

Cass, H. and P. Holford. *Natural Highs: Feel Good All the Time.* New York, NY: Avery, 2002.

Chen, T. J., K. Blum, A. L. Chen, A. Bowirrat, W. B. Downs, M. A. Madigan, R. L. Waite, J. A. Bailey, M. Kerner, S. Yeldandi, N. Majmundar, J. Giordano, S. Morse, D. Miller, F. Fornari, and E. R. Braverman. "Neurogenetics and Clinical Evidence for the Putative Activation of the Brain Reward Circuitry by a Neuroadaptagen: Proposing an Addiction

Candidate Gene Panel Map." *J Psychoactive Drugs* 43 no. 2 (2011): 108–27.

Chen, A. L., K. Blum, T. J. Chen, J. Giordano, B. W. Downs, D. Han, D. Barh, and E. R. Braverman. "Correlation of the Taq1 Dopamine D2 Receptor Gene and Percent Body Fat in Obese and Screened Control Subjects: A Preliminary Report." *Journal of Food & Function* 3 no. 1, 40–8.

Childre, D. and H. Martin. *The Heartmath Solution*. New York, NY: HarperOne, 1999.

Dinubile, N., W. Westcott, G. Reinl, A. Balai, E. R. Braverman, M. Madigan, J. Giordano, and K. Blum. "MarcProTM Device a Novel Paradigm Shift in Muscle Conditioning, Recovery and Performance: Induction of Nitric Oxide (NO) Dependent Enhanced Microcirculation Coupled with Angiogenesis Mechanisms." *Journal of Exercise Physiology Online* 14 no. 5 (2011): 10–19.

Fisher, G. and T. Harrison. *Substance Abuse: Information for Schools Counselors, Social Workers, Therapists, and Counselors*. New York, NY: Allyn & Bacon, 2005.

Gamblers Anonymous. *A Day at a Time Los Angeles*. CA: Gamblers Anonymous, 2007.

Overeaters Anonymous. *Overeaters Anonymous.* Rio Rancho, NM: Overeaters Anonymous Incorporated, 2001.

Gant, C. and K. Hurley. "105 Patients Heavy Metal Results." Presented at Holistic Treatment: Changing the Way We Look at Recovery: Mind Body and Spirit. Las Vegas, NV (2010).

Gant, C. and K. Hurley. *End Your Nicotine Addiction Now.* Miami, FL: Mind Mender Press, 2011.

Gorski, T. and M. Miller. *Staying Sober: A Guide for Relapse Prevention.* Independence, MO: Herald House/Independence Press, 1986.

Harch, P. and V. McCullough. *The Oxygen Revolution.* New York, NY: Hatherleigh Press, 2007.

Hurley, K. and L. Pasqua. *Rebooting the Brain Without Sugar, Drugs or Alcohol.* Naples, FL: Nutritional Health Choices Inc, 2012.

Hurley, K., L. Pasqua, and S. Morse. *Brain Interrupted.* In press, 2012.

Hurnard, H. *Hinds Feet on High Places.* Shippensburg, PA: Destiny Image Publishers, 2005.

Larson, J. M. *Seven Weeks to Sobriety*, New York, NY: Ballantine Books, 1997.

Marx, R. *It's Not Your Fault: Overcoming Anorexia and Bulimia through Biopsychiatry.* New York, NY: Villard, 1991.

Mellody, P. *Facing Love Addiction: Giving Yourself the Power to Change the Way You Love.* New York, NY : HarperOne, 1992.

Miller, D. and K. Blum. *Overload.* Innsbrook, MO: Miller Associates, 2000.

Miller, M. and D. Miller. *Staying Clean & Sober: Complementary and Natural Strategies for Healing the Addicted Brain.* Orem, UT: Woodland Publishing, 2005.

Miller, M., A. Chen, S. Stokes, S. Silverman, A. Bowirrat, M. Manka, Ma. Manka, D. Miller, K. Kenneth, T. Chen, J. Bailey, B. Downs, D. Waite, M. Madigan, E. Braverman, U. Damle, M. Kerner, J. Giordano, M. Oscar-Berman, and K. Blum. "Early Intervention of Intravenous KB220IV- Neuroadaptagen Amino-Acid Therapy (NAAT)™ Improves Behavioral Outcomes in a Residential Addiction Treatment Program: A Pilot Study." *Journal of Substance Abuse Treatment.* 2011.

Millman, D. *Way of the Peaceful Warrior.* Tiburon, CA: HJ Kramer, 2006.

Morse, S., J. Giordano. K. Perrine, B. W. Downs, R. L. Waite, M. Madigan, J. Bailey, E. R. Braverman, U. Damle, T. Simpatico, M. D. Moelelr, and K. Blum. "Audio Therapy Significantly Attenuates Aberrant Mood in Residential Patient Addiction Treatment: Putative Activation of Dopaminergic Pathways in the Meso-Limbic Reward Circuitry of Humans." *Journal of Addiction Therapy.* In review.

Narcotics Anonymous. *It Works: How and Why.* Chatsworth, CA: Narcotics Anonymous World Service, 1993.

Narcotics Anonymous. *Narcotics Anonymous.* 6th ed. Chatsworth, CA: Narcotics Anonymous World Service, 2008.

Norden, M. *Beyond Prozac: Brain-Toxic Lifestyles, Natural Antidotes and New Generation Antidepressants.* New York, NY: HarperCollins Publishers, 1996.

Redfield, J. *The Celestine Prophecy.* Boston, MA:Warner Books Inc., 1997.

Ross, J. *The Diet Cure.* New York, NY: Penguin, 2000.

Ross, J. *The Mood Cure*. New York, NY: Viking Adult, 2002.

Sex and Love Addicts Anonymous. *Sex and Love Addicts Anonymous*. San Antnio, TX: Augustine Fellowship, 1986.

Trungpa, C. *Shambhala the Sacred Path of the Warrior*. C. R. Gimian (ed.). Boston, MA: Shambhala (1988).

Waite, R. L., C. Allen, J. Giordano, S. Morse, A. Bowirrat, B. W. Downs, M. Madigan, E. R. Braverman, M. Kerner, J. Bailey, and K. Blum. "Quantitative Electroencephalography Analysis (qEEG) of Neuro-Electro-Adaptive Therapy 12" [NEAT12] Up-Regulates Cortical Potentials in an Alcoholic during Protracted Abstinence: Putative Anti-Craving Implications." *Journal of Medical Case Reports*. In review.

Werback, M. R. *Nutritional Influences on Mental Illness*. Tarzana, CA: Third Line Press, 1991.

Werback, M. R. *Foundations of Nutritional Medicine*. Tarzana, CA: Third Line Press, 1997.

Westcott, W. L., T. Chen, F. B. Neric, N. DiNubile, A. Bowirrat, M. Madigan, B. W. Downs, J. Giordano, S. Morse, A. L. Chen, A. Bajaj,

M. Kerner, E. Braverman, G. Reinl, and M. Blakemore, S. Whitehead, L. Sacks, and K. Blum. "The Marc ProTM Device Improves Muscle Performance and Recovery From Concentric and Eccentric Exercise Induced Muscle Fatigue In Humans: A Pilot Study." *Journal of Exercise Physiology Online* 14 no. 2 (2011): 55–67.

Westcott, W., J. Varghesse, N. Dinubile, N. Moynih, R. L. Loud, S. Whitehead, S. Brothers, J. Giordano, S. Morse, M. Madigan, and K. Blum. "Exercise and Nutrition More Effective than Exercise Alone for Increasing Lean Weight and Reducing Resting Blood Pressure." *Journal of Exercise Physiologistsonline* 14 no. 4 (2011): 120–33.

INSIGHTS INTO YOUR "OTHER" BRAIN

Could the source of your anxiety and depression be coming from your gut – the answer may surprise you!

You've probably heard or even used one of these phrases or a variation; "I have butterflies in my stomach," "it gives me a pit in my stomach" or "I've got a gut feeling about this." Pretty common clichés, right? What most people are unaware of is that the sensations they speak of are real and generated in the same place as the feeling itself, in our gut.

For ages scientists and doctors have been aware of our 'second' brain, but are just beginning to understand its full impact. They now believe that a lot of what makes us human depends on microbial activity in the gut.

Clinically known as the Enteric Nervous System – or ENS for short – this system has approximately 500 million neurons (a specialized cell transmitting nerve impulses), or five times as many neurons found in the spinal cord and about one two-hundredth of the number in the brain. The extensive amount of neurons allows us to "feel" the inner world of our gut and its contents. ENS also contributes to our level of anxiety, appetite, satiety, our mood, emotions, learning, memory and overall inflammation.

In his article titled "Your Backup Brain" published in Psychology Today, Dan Hurley explains the Enteric Nervous System this way: "Think of yourself as the biological equivalent of a doughnut, with the inner lining of your intestines, the doughnut hole, facing an "inner" external world— food, water, bacteria, and whatever else you swallow—just as your skin faces the "outer" external world. While your ears, eyes, and sense of touch permit you to see, hear, and feel the outer exterior of your body, the intestines employ the ENS to sense, manipulate, and respond to the inner exterior, the doughnut hole of your gut."

ENS is a complex mesh-like system of neurons that lines the gastrointestinal system all the way from the esophagus to the anus which measures about thirty-feet end to end. It controls the movement and absorption of food throughout the intestines. ENS also communicates with brain via the vagus nerve which extends from the brainstem to your visceral organs. This channel, known as the gut-brain axis, connects the emotional and cognitive centers of the brain with intestinal function, and vice-versa. Some of these messages from the gut can directly affect our mood, behavior, feelings of sadness or stress and decision-making.

Our gastrointestinal system also contains a complex community of over 100 trillion microbial cells. These microorganisms join together to form a community known as a microbiome, also known as Gut Flora. These colonies influence our physiology, metabolism, nutrition and immune function. Disruptions to the gut microbiome have been linked to gastrointestinal conditions such as inflammatory bowel disease and obesity.

Although the exact mechanisms remain elusive, scientists have been able to prove through functional magnetic resonance imaging or functional MRI (fMRI) that your gut and your emotions are linked directly together. They were also able to show a connection between the gut and the prefrontal cortex, an area of the brain associated with planning complex cognitive behavior, personality expression, decision making, and moderating social behavior.

Mark Lyte Ph.D is one of the world's leading experts on microbial endocrinology (the union of neurobiology and microbiology). He has spent the last 25 years researching the subject. Dr. Lyte found that micro-organisms in our gut secrete chemicals – among them are dopamine, serotonin and gamma-aminobutyric acid (GABA). These are the very same neurotransmitters produced in the brain that communicate a sense of calm and ease. They regulate mood and are often referred to as the 'feel good' chemicals. It was once believed that these chemicals could not cross the blood/brain barrier. However, that belief is not on the stable ground it once was.

Although the research is limited, it appears as though the dopamine, serotonin and GABA in the gut has a role in intestinal disorders that coincides with high levels of major depression and anxiety. A recent study conducted by a research group in Norway revealed that certain bacteria were more likely to be associated with depressive patients.

With over 100 trillion microbial cells in our gastrointestinal system it is easy to see that this is one very complex system. It is estimated that over 40,000,000 million people suffer from some form of gastrointestinal disorder every year. Sadly, most cases go undiagnosed and untreated.

For example, let's take a look at leaky gut syndrome. WEBMD calls it a medical mystery. Gastroenterologist Donald Kirby, MD, director of the Center for Human

Nutrition at the Cleveland Clinic says, "From an MD's standpoint, it's a very gray area. Physicians don't know enough about the gut, which is our biggest immune system organ."

Leaky gut syndrome isn't a diagnosis taught in medical school. Instead, leaky gut really means you've got a diagnosis that still needs to be made. You hope that your doctor is a good-enough Sherlock Holmes, but sometimes it is very hard to make a diagnosis."

Linda A. Lee, MD, a gastroenterologist and director of the Johns Hopkins Integrative Medicine and Digestive Center added this, "We don't know a lot but we know that it exists. In the absence of evidence, we don't know what it means or what therapies can directly address it." I don't know about you, but statements like these from top line physicians and researchers do not distill much confidence in me regarding our current healthcare model.

Leaky gut syndrome is a condition where the intestinal lining has became more porous, with more holes developing that are larger in size. Consequently, the screening out process is no longer functioning properly. The result is undigested food molecules and other "bad stuff" including – but not limited to – yeast, toxins, and all other forms of waste, flows freely into the bloodstream. This triggers an immune system response, inflammation, while sending a stress/anxiety signal to the brain. Gone untreated, the prolonged stress/anxiety message will deplete dopamine, serotonin and other neurotransmitters in the brain that are linked to depression. As most of you already know, there is a direct connection between depression and substance/alcohol abuse.

I find this particularly alarming taking into consideration the number of chemicals being added to our food supply that can disrupt our Enteric Nervous System. Twenty-years ago the FDA succumbed to the pressures of the food industry lobby and – in its infinite wisdom – put the food industry on the honor system. The change in policy allowed the food industry to determine whether or not a food additive is 'Generally Recognized As Safe (GRAS)' and are not legally required to notify the FDA of a GRAS determination.

In other words, the FDA took the chains off of the food industry and relinquished any and all forms of control over bad actors. This policy opened the door for rabid, profit-starved CEOs to put just about anything they want into our foods and call it safe without fear of retribution. What could possibly go wrong?!

The effects of this decision were felt immediately and there seems to be no limit to what the food industry will add to our food supply in the name of profits. Today, you can find the exact same chemical used to manufacture athletic shoe soles in hot dog and hamburger buns on the shelves in chain super markets and all the popular fast food restaurants across the country. All these years you've had your foot in your mouth and didn't even realize it. The FDA and the USDA approved the industrial chemical azodicarbonamide for use in food as a bleaching agent and dough conditioner even though it has been linked to cancer.

Europe and Australia have banned this dangerous chemical. However, here in the U.S. there are over 500 foods that azodicarbonamide can be found in. You simply can avoid it.

This is just one small example that I bring to your attention to help you realize just how pervasive dangerous toxins have become in our food supply. There are literally thousands of other examples I could have used. In fact, there are over 10,000 chemicals, drugs, and formulations in our food and environment that the FDA and USDA have absolutely no idea how they will collectively and/or independently affect our health and well-being. The whole situation makes me want to put on a Bio Hazmet Suit before I go to the grocery store – or at least a lab coat with protective glasses and rubber gloves.

If you want to get your anxiety and depression under control I'd strongly recommend that you contact me (786-271-5732) or a reputable integrative medicine doctor such as Dr. Hyla Cass (https://cassmd.com/) and ask them to develop a plan that fits your lifestyle. All things considered, this is not an expensive proposition that can improve your quality of life and may just save it.

A FIX FOR DEPRESSION, ANXIETY AND ADVERSE BEHAVIORS

Don't accept what I'm saying without Googling it!

- Get tested for food allergies.
- Avoid foods that cause inflammation such as wheat, dairy, refined sugar, fried foods, caffeine, alcohol and GMO foods.
- Eat foods high in fiber.
- Eat healthy fats that can be found in fish, olive and coconut oils, avocados and flax.
- A steady regimen of enzymes, prebiotics and probiotics is recommended to get your depression and anxiety under control (remember there are more serotonin receptors in your gut than in your brain. Serotonin is one of the 'feel good' chemicals our body produces.).
- Adding the amino acid supplement L-glutamine to your daily regime will aid in rejuvenating the lining of the intestinal wall.